DATE DUE

F.61

Social Ends and Political Means

Social Ends and Political Means

edited by

TED HONDERICH

Department of Philosophy,
University College London

Routledge & Kegan Paul
London, Henley and Boston

First published in 1976
by Routledge & Kegan Paul Ltd
39 Store Street
London WC1E 2DD,
Newtown Road,
Henley-on-Thames,
Oxon RG9 1EN, and
9 Park Street,
Boston, Mass. 02108, USA
Set in 11/12 pt Monotype Plantin
and printed in Great Britain by
Butler & Tanner Ltd
Frome and London

ISBN 0 7100 8370 X

Contents

Preface

These are new essays which have to do with better societies than we have and the means of getting them. They are essays which exemplify real political philosophy. That is, they are in that assertive tradition of thought whose past makers have been Plato, Hobbes, Locke, Rousseau, Hegel, Mill and Marx. All of these philosophers, whatever their other concerns, were mainly engaged in advancing and defending conceptions of acceptable societies or of acceptable ways of achieving them. They were not outside or above ordinary moral and political dispute about conditions of human existence. Still, while this book has in it no politically withdrawn scholar's analysis of the general idea of the state, no seemingly neutral discussion of the coherence of socialism, and no second-order inquiry into the nature of political theory itself, none of the essays is mere affirmation, let alone declamation. They are not manifestos. All of them proceed to conclusions only by way of analysis and argument of one decent kind or another.

They do not come together into a chorus. About half of them are Marxist and about half derive from opposed or anyway different commitments, all of which may be described, in a very general way indeed, as liberal. The latter description can be used of them, of course, only because of its encompassing vagueness. There would, I think, be an essay of a more conservative character than there is if all philosophers found writing down the truth, in a certain time, only about as difficult as promising to do so. The Marxist essays, taken by themselves, are not a chorus either. They show national differences but that is but a beginning. Several of them express views which have played a part in the censure of their authors and in fact in punitive action taken against them. It is very satisfactory to have them in the book.

As will be plain enough, the choice of essays derives in good part from the persuasion that diverse opinions should be heard. This persuasion derives in good part from the conviction of our common fallibility. John Stuart Mill, in *On Liberty*, provided a

vii

fervent defence of the argument from fallibility to the free expression of opinion. He did not say so much as he might have of the necessary uncertainty of our judgment about methods and modes of reflection, as distinct from conclusions drawn. It is true, of course, that there is no shortage of writing which one can dismiss, without hesitation, as failing to come up to bottom standards of clarity, judgment and order. There remains much argument, to speak a bit parochially, of which philosophers in the British analytic and empirical tradition take leave too readily. Certainly with respect to political philosophy, there is too much confident assumption about the worth and the worthlessness of different methods and modes of reflection.

What remains to be said about the book, before turning to more particular introduction of the essays and their authors, is that not all of the essays are of a general character. Not all of them, that is, offer a general characterization of a society we ought to have or a general account of the way or ways of proceeding toward it. Several of them take up aspects of these questions. There is room, needless to say, for both the more and the less general.

It is perhaps reassuring that there has seemed to be no plain and obvious way of ordering or grouping the essays. Not all of them are expressly about either political means or social ends. And, if several of them do concentrate in this way, it is obvious that all the essays have at least implications about answers to both questions. The essays which come first, as I have finally ordered them, have rather more to do with means, and, perhaps naturally, are also those which have been roughly described as of a liberal kind. Those which come second are of Marxist commitment and pertain more to ends.

R. M. Hare's essay bears directly on the question of what constraints we are under in attempting to change society. Whether we consider the democratic method narrowly conceived, or activism or resistance, or revolutionary action, there is the matter of what has traditionally been called our political obligation. Professor Hare is concerned with its analysis and its grounds. He specifies political obligations as those particular moral obligations that lie upon us because we are citizens of a state with laws. His reasoning, which has its beginning in the theory of moral language and argument which is owed to him, depends in part on a relevant analogy and comes to a conclusion of a utilitarian nature.

The ideal of free speech pertains both to means of change and to ends. In his essay Stephen Norris distinguishes, within the ideal of free speech, the separate ideals of equal speech and freedom of opinion. The first has to do with who expresses an opinion, the second with the opinion itself. Mill's arguments, whatever his hope, are discovered to be of the wrong kind to support the ideal of equal speech, and the ideal itself is judged to be dubious. As for freedom of opinion, both its scope and foundation are claimed to need reconsideration.

Another ideal, that of respect for persons, with persons conceived not as they sometimes are, but as all individuals who make claims and demands, or on whose behalf claims and demands are made, governs Edward Kent's discussion. He is concerned with the authoritarian character of contemporary societies and the need for a further development of identity-groups within societies. Such groups, of different kinds, are regarded as essential to effective social protest, and they are equally essential to the good society to be gained through protest.

The essay by L. J. Macfarlane is closest of all those in the book to the actuality of politics, in particular the actuality of political confrontation. Dr Macfarlane sets out an analytic description of attitudes which have to do with and which enter into a clash between a community's police and civil rights marchers. His minute analysis is relevant to certain hypotheses about authority in society, and hence to our obligations.

Rights of persons, those once called natural rights, are the subject of the essay by Ruth Anna Putnam. Social progress has been made by way of claims of these rights, she grants, despite certain obscurities and confusions. Such claims, however, and the tradition which contains them, that of liberalism, have ceased to be things of fundamental importance. Liberalism now rests on false assumptions, and cannot serve our progress.

Lucio Colletti deals in his essay with the Marxist prediction of the collapse of capitalism and an ensuing order of society. In order to do so, he considers Marx's responses to the utopian socialists, so-called, and to the classical political economists. Each of these responses has to do with Marx's commitment to revolution and his general theory of capitalism and history.

Adam Schaff begins with instances of alienation, in which products of several kinds escape the intentions of their makers, and the related phenomenon of auto-alienation, which is primarily a matter of the subjective experience of individuals. The theory of alienation is found to have its origin in the thought of Marx, while opposition to the theory, on the part of 'orthodox' Marxists and others, is found to have its origin in the fact among others that alienation is not a phenomenon peculiar to capitalist societies.

Socialist self-management, as expounded by Mihailo Marković, is related to but different from workers' control, participatory democracy, direct democracy, decentralization, and the dictatorship of the proletariat. Marković sets out the nature of socialist self-management, discusses its philosophical basis, and defends its feasibility. His is one of the essays which has in it a general conception of a preferable society.

One relationship between the communist and his party, that of unlimited party commitment, is for Svetozar Stojanović destructive of the dignity of the communist. It is a relationship which is beyond the limit of revolutionary self-sacrifice. He discusses its connection with the doctrine of the 'objective' meaning of actions, and 'objective' guilt, and examines its consequences for the revolutionary goal of a society in which there can be a full development of the human personality.

R. M. Hare, White's Professor of Moral Philosophy in the University of Oxford, is the author of *The Language of Morals, Freedom and Reason, Practical Inferences, Essays on Philosophical Method, Essays on the Moral Concepts* and *Applications of Moral Philosophy*.

Stephen E. Norris is a young American philosopher, now teaching at the University of Missouri at St Louis, and the author of several philosophical essays.

Edward Kent is a professor of philosophy at the City University of New York, the author of a number of philosophical essays and the editor of *Law and Philosophy* and *Revolution and the Rule of Law*.

L. J. Macfarlane, Fellow and Tutor in Politics at St John's College, Oxford, is the author of *Modern Political Theory, Political Disobedience* and *Violence and the State*.

Ruth Anna Putnam, a professor of philosophy at Wellesley College, Mass., is the author of essays in the philosophy of science and in political philosophy.

Lucio Colletti, Reader in the History of Philosophy at Rome University and Professor of the History of Philosophy at the University of Salerno, is the author of a number of books on Marxism, including *From Rousseau to Lenin: Studies in Ideology and Society*.

Adam Schaff, now president of the European Centre for the Social Sciences in Vienna, and a member of the Polish Academy of

Sciences, has been Professor of Philosophy at Warsaw University and a member of the Central Committee of the Polish United Workers Party. His books include *Introduction to Semantics*, *A Philosophy of Man* and *Marxism and the Human Individual*.

Mihailo Marković has been Director of the Institute of Philosophy in the University of Belgrade and is the author of a number of books, including *Formalism in Contemporary Logic*, *Dialectic and Humanism*, and *Re-examinations*.

Svetozar Stojanović has been Professor of Moral and Political Philosophy at the University of Belgrade and is the author of *Between Ideals and Reality: A Critique of Socialism and Its Future* and also *Contemporary Meta-Ethics*.

My thanks are due to my colleague, G. A. Cohen, for his good advice in connection with this book, and to Dinah Perry for exemplary editorial assistance.

T.H.

1 Political Obligation

R. M. HARE

This paper is one of a number of essays which I have written in recent years on the application of ethical theory to practical issues.[1] The objects of all these have been the same; first to do something for the morally perplexed, including myself – the aim with which I originally became a moral philosopher; secondly, to gain greater insight into the theory itself by seeing how it works in practice; and thirdly, to convince the prejudiced and obtuse majority of my profession that a formal ethical theory about the logical properties of the moral concepts, which itself begs no questions of moral substance, and can therefore be accepted by people of differing moral opinions, can shed light on practical questions, and lead in practice to their solution. It is not my purpose here to defend my views about these logical properties, but only their relevance to practice if true. Those readers who question my theoretical assumptions will have to look elsewhere for their justification.[2]

The expression 'political obligation', although it conveniently delimits my topic, ought not to be used (though it often is) without an awareness of its dangers. As I shall use the term, political obligation is not (as perhaps legal obligation is) a species of the genus obligation, co-ordinate with moral obligation; it is, rather, a sub-species of moral obligation, co-ordinate with other sub-species such as social and parental obligations. Just as parental obligations are the *moral* obligations which we incur when we become parents (for example to feed our children) and social

© R. M. Hare 1976

1 Others are: *Freedom and Reason*, ch. 11 (on racial conflict); *Ph. and Pub. Aff.*, 1, 1972 (on war) and 4, 1975 (on abortion); and contributions to *Nature and Conduct*, ed. R. Peters (on environmental planning) and to *New Essays in the Philosophy of Education*, ed. G. Langford and D. J. O'Connor (on moral education); and many of the papers in my *Applications of Moral Philosophy*.

2 See especially my books *The Language of Morals*, *Freedom and Reason*, and *Essays on the Moral Concepts*, and my papers 'Principles' (*Ar. Soc.*, lxxii, 1972/3 and 'Ethical Theory and Utilitarianism' in *Contemporary British Philosophy 4*, ed. H. D. Lewis.

1

obligations the *moral* obligations that we have because we are
members of a society, so political obligations are the *moral* obligations that lie upon us because we are citizens (*politai*) of a state
with laws. To think that political obligations are, not a sub-
species of moral obligations, but a species of the genus obligation
(if there is one) co-ordinate with moral obligations, might lead
someone to do highly immoral acts in the name of a 'political
obligation' conceived of as overriding morality; but, if we ask
what such a 'political obligation' could be, or what could be its
source, the resulting darkness may persuade us that this way of
using the terms is radically misconceived. Be that as it may, I
shall myself be speaking only of those *moral* obligations that we
have because we are citizens, and of how they arise.

Does the fact that I am a citizen of the United Kingdom lay
upon me moral obligations which I should not have if I were not?
Most people think that it does: obligations, not only to obey the
laws of the United Kingdom in general (there may be exceptions)
but to take part in the political process in order to improve those
laws if they need it, to defend them if they do not, and, in general,
to perform the 'duty of a citizen'. I shall be concentrating in the
main on one of these kinds of obligation, the moral obligation to
obey the laws – although I acknowledge that this obligation may
lie, not only on citizens, but also on anybody, even an alien,
who finds himself within the jurisdiction (most people think that
foreign visitors too have a moral obligation not to steal). This
moral obligation to obey the laws must of course be distinguished
from legal obligations (i.e. the requirements, morality aside, of the
laws themselves). That there is a legal obligation in a certain
country to serve in the army does not entail that there is a moral
obligation to obey the law imposing this legal obligation; a person
who said that there was not would not be contradicting himself,
even if he admitted that that was the law.

One source of confusion must be removed at the outset. It might
be argued that, because moral principles have to be universal, the
expression 'the United Kingdom' cannot occur in one. And
from this it might be concluded that I cannot have any duties
qua citizen of, or resident in, the United Kingdom. This is a
simple mistake. The moral principle involved does not contain
any singular terms like 'The United Kingdom'; it contains universal relational terms such as 'resident in' or 'citizen of'. Such a
principle might be, for example, the following: 'One ought to
obey the laws of the country of which one is a citizen, unless one

or other of the following conditions is satisfied, etc.'. From this, in conjunction with the premiss that I am a citizen of the United Kingdom, I can derive the conclusion that I have a duty to obey the laws of the United Kingdom, unless, etc.; but the moral principle itself does not contain this singular term.

How, then, do political obligations arise? Attempts have been made in the past to show that they arise because we have assumed contractual obligations through becoming citizens. It is now generally acknowledged that the social contract is a fiction to which no reality corresponds; there has been no contract. However, as a matter of philosophical history, Rousseau, who put forward such a theory, greatly influenced the moral philosophy of Kant, who gave as helpful an account of the nature of morality as anybody could who wrote in such an impenetrably obscure style. My own view, which owes a lot to Kant, might therefore be said to contain traces of Rousseau, as does that of Professor Rawls.[1]

Sooner than speak of a fictitious or hypothetical contract, however, it is clearer to start directly from the logical properties of the moral concepts. If I am right about these, to ask what obligations I have as citizen is to ask for a universal prescription applicable to all people who are citizens of a country in circumstances just like those in which I find myself. That is to say, I have to ask – as in *any* case when faced with a question about what I morally ought to do – 'What universal principle of action can I accept for cases just like this, disregarding the fact that I occupy the place in the situation that I do (i.e. giving no preferential weight to my own interests just because they are mine)?' This will lead me to give equal weight to the equal interests of every individual affected by my actions, and thus to accept the principle which will in all most promote those interests. Thus I am led to a form of utilitarianism.[2]

For political, as for other, obligations we could ask this universal-prescriptive question directly of each individual case, and no general principles would be required, although, in deciding on

---

1 For the analogies and differences between Rawls's theory and my own, see my review articles on his *Theory of Justice* in *Ph.Q.* 23, 1973; *Ph. and Pub. Aff.*, 1, 1972, pp. 167–71; and B. Barry, *The Liberal Theory of Justice*, pp. 12 f. Barry is right in his conjecture that my *Freedom and Reason* was not directly influenced by Rawls's views; I did not see the similarity between them and it until after it was written, and in particular after reading, in typescript, D. A. J. Richards's *Theory of Reasons for Action*.

2 Rawls would be led to the same conclusion by his own method if he abjured intuitions which are not justified by the method; see my review in *Ph.Q.* just cited.

each case, we would be accepting some *universal* principle.[1]
Thus in theory no distinction between *'prima facie'* obligations
(which are expressed in simple, general rules) and 'actual' obligations is needed. But in practice it is not only useful but necessary
to have some simple, general and more or less unbreakable
principles, both for the purposes of moral education and self-
education (i.e. character-formation), and to keep us from special
pleadings and other errors when in situations of ignorance or
stress. Even when we have such principles, we *could* disregard
them in an individual case and reason it out *ab initio*; but it is
nearly always dangerous to do so, as well as impracticable; impracticable, because we are unlikely to have either the time or the
information, and dangerous, because we shall almost inevitably
cheat, and cook up the case until we can reach a conclusion palatable
to ourselves. The general principle that we ought to obey the law is
a strong candidate for inclusion in such a list, as I shall be trying
to show; there may be occasions for breaking it, but the principle
is one which in general there is good reason for inculcating in
ourselves and others.

In order to apply all this to politics, let us start with a very simple
model of the political situation. Suppose that a hundred of us are
cast away on a desert island. At once moral questions will arise
owing to the fact that our actions affect the interests of the others.
The answers to these questions will be given by what will most
promote the interests of those affected by our actions (including
ourselves, but not giving ourselves a privileged position). It will be
seen that some of these questions can be answered without bringing in any reference to politics or to laws – which may not yet
exist. For example, I have a duty to observe hygiene, because, if
I do not, people will die of diseases as a result of my negligence, and
the satisfaction of interests will therefore not be maximized. To
take a specific instance; I have a duty to wash and delouse myself
regularly to prevent the spread of typhus. On the other hand,
some obligations arise only because of the existence or possible
existence of laws. I shall call those obligations which arise independently of the existence of laws or of a state, *social* obligations;
they arise if people are living together in a society, whether or not

---

1 For the too much neglected distinction between universality and
generality in principles, see my paper 'Principles' (*Ar. Soc.*, lxxii, 1972/3).
For the terms *'prima facie'* and 'actual' see Sir David Ross, *The Right and
the Good* (1930), pp. 19 f.

that society is organized politically into a state with laws. And I shall call the obligations which arise only because there is a state with laws, *political* obligations.

As an example of the latter kind of obligations, consider obligations relating to the possession of goods (obligations which would concern matters of property and ownership, *if* we had the legal institution of property on our island). Let us suppose that I have in my possession enough food for myself and to spare for a few weeks, and so have a number of others; but some people have nothing. We might well say that if no laws are in contemplation, I shall be best serving the interests of people in general if I allow my own store to be divided up. But I shall then have no assurance that this benevolent action of mine will be imitated by others who have food. And, I might reason, what is my little store among so many? I should promote people's interests still more if I could bring it about, by an exercise of leadership, that there is set up a law, enacted perhaps by acclamation at a town meeting and enforced by volunteer policemen, *regulating* the distribution of the available food. It is not self-evident that the law will, if the people at the town meeting decide rationally and impartially in the interests of all, require the *equal* distribution of food. It may be that, because of the difficulty of enforcing the law and avoiding concealment, they will agree to those who have stores keeping part of them so long as they hand over part for distribution. It may be, also, that extra food will be allowed to those who need it in order to preserve their strength so that they can go out fishing or cultivate the land. Or it may be that extra rations will be offered as an incentive to suitable people to get them to produce food in these ways. It may even be that a system of competition, with currency and a market, will be adopted in order to spur people on to maximize their production of food. Such a system relies on laws, both to establish the currency (though barter might do, and this is in any case not the most important reason), and to secure to people the property which they have got for themselves by competition (for otherwise there will be no incentive to compete).

It is not my intention to attempt a comparative evaluation of these different economic systems. But I take it as obvious that the general interests of people in society will be promoted by having *some* laws regulating property and the distribution of goods. Some legal systems will promote these interests better than others; but almost any system of laws that has much chance of getting adopted is likely to promote them better than having no laws at all.

And the same holds good of other laws relating to such matters as hygiene (which I have mentioned already), the settlement of disputes and the avoidance of violence. Anarchy, as those know who have experienced it, is seldom in the general interest. But one can also have *too many* laws.

I could have mentioned other laws too. There would probably be one requiring the able-bodied to arm themselves as well as they can and turn out to repel aggressors from neighbouring islands. But the points I now wish to make can best be illustrated by reference to hygiene. We saw that even without any laws I had some obligation to observe cleanly habits. But the enactment of hygiene laws adds to this obligation. If we can see why it adds to it, we shall understand a great deal about the obligation to keep the law. It adds to it, not because the mere enactment by the town meeting of a law lays any moral obligation on me directly, but because it alters the conditions under which I am asking my moral question.

How does it alter these conditions? Primarily by bringing it about that observance of hygiene by me has more chance of achieving its purposes, because other people, who would not of their own accord observe hygiene, are being coerced into doing so. Before the law is enacted and enforced, if I keep myself clear of lice I am not making very much difference to the number of lice biting other people. This is because, owing to general apathy, there are a great many lice about. I may not be very successful in getting even myself deloused, if we are living at close quarters. But if there is an enforced law which makes nearly all the others, from fear of the penalty, delouse themselves, *my* delousing or not delousing myself makes a much bigger difference to the hygiene of people in general. Consider the extreme case: everyone else has deloused themselves for fear of the penalty, and I alone have lice, and for some reason think I can escape detection. Let us suppose that besides having lice I am a typhus carrier, or that there is one sleeping near me. Then it is obvious that my failure to delouse myself will make a *very great* difference to the likelihood of people getting typhus; and thus my obligation to do so (because it is in the general interest) will be much greater than it would be if there were no law, and therefore little delousing, and therefore the epidemic was going to spread whatever I did.

We may now sum up the results of this unsavoury discussion by tabulating the reasons which I have so far acquired for obeying the hygiene laws. There are, first of all,

A. *Prudential Reasons* (ignored in what follows)

  A.*1* My own interest in not getting bitten by lice or catching typhus;

  A.*2* My own interest in not incurring the legal penalty for lousiness, with the public opprobrium entailed.

Note that A.*1* owes nothing to the existence of the law, whereas A*2* owes something but not everything.

B. *Moral Reasons not related to the existence of the law*

  B.*1* The fact that failure to delouse myself will, law or no law, harm people's interests by making them *a little* more likely to get lice or typhus;

  B.*2* The fact that if I myself get typhus I shall be a burden to others;

C. *Moral Reasons related to the existence of the law*

  C.*1* The fact that, because there is an enforced law, resulting in general delousing, failure to delouse myself will harm people's interests much more, by making them *very much* more likely to get lice or typhus;

  C.*2* The fact that, if I break this law, it will cause trouble to the police in catching me, thus rendering necessary the employment of more policemen, who therefore cannot grow yams instead, and so harming the interests of the people who could have eaten the yams;

  C.*3* The fact that, if I break this law, it may encourage people to break this or other laws, thereby rendering a little more likely (*a*) the removal of the benefits to society which come from the existence of those particular laws, and (*b*) the breakdown of the rule of law altogether, which would do great harm to the interests of nearly everybody.

Only the reasons given under *C* (the last three) lay upon me *political* obligations; and of them, the second and third are subsidiary, but have the important property that (except for C.*3*(*a*)) they might survive even if the law in question were a bad or unnecessary one whose existence did not promote the general interest. To these must be added at least one other kind of political obligation, mentioned already, namely the obligation to further the enactment and enforcement of good laws – an obligation which arises because it is in the interests of people in general, including myself, that I should do this. I leave out of consideration the case of the person in whose interest it is that there should not be laws (because he can do better for himself without them). He is not relevant, because we are considering the question, what I morally ought to do, and to answer *this* question I have to treat others' interests as of equal weight to my own. If this fortunate person does that, he will come to the same answers as we have come to.

I have listed one major, and two subsidiary, moral reasons for obeying the law. There may well be others. And the hygiene example may not be typical. Do the same considerations apply, for instance, to laws about property? It might be argued that they do not, as has been suggested to me by Dr Honderich.

It must at any rate be allowed that, if there were no laws of property, there could be no theft; for theft can only be of property, and there is no property without laws – at least customary laws – about possessions. So *if* there is a moral obligation not to steal, it owes its existence to law, as a necessary constitutive condition of the institution of property. The question is, however, whether, given the existence of this institution and its constitutive laws, there is in general a moral obligation to abstain from breaking them. According to the utilitarian there will be, if breaking them is in general likely to harm the interests of people in society.

It might be thought that thefts do not harm the interests of anybody except the victim, and that if he is rich and the thief poor, the diminishing marginal utility of goods will in most cases bring it about that the theft creates a net gain in utility. But this is to leave out of account the side-effects of stealing. The more thefts there are, the more precautions people and the state will take against theft; and the cost, both financial and other, of the precautions (the cost of the police force, of locks and banks, the inconvenience and unpleasantness of having to watch one's property or go in fear of losing it and the growth of general mistrust) is likely to outweigh the utilities created by theft. On the other hand, if precautions are not taken, theft will become so general that the whole institution of property will collapse. Only those, therefore, who think this institution unnecessary for the general welfare will be able to prescribe that everybody who wants to should steal.

But this in itself does not quite restore the analogy with the hygiene case. It is true that we could represent the spread of theft as analogous to an epidemic; but a single theft could never have the same effect in spreading it as a single typhus-carrying louse in my clothing might. Readers of such books as Professor Lyons's *Forms and Limits of Utilitarianism* will be familiar with examples in which one person can, by breaking a law, secure for himself an advantage at the cost of no comparable disadvantage to others, because he knows that they are all going to keep the law, and it takes quite a large number of breaches of it to produce any substantial disutility. A common example is that of the person who uses electricity for space-heating contrary to Government orders in a power shortage, knowing that others are too law-abiding to do likewise, and that he will not be detected. He gets the warmth, and no power stations break down, because he is one of only a very few delinquents. Utility is therefore increased by this action which most of us would condemn; and so utilitarianism seems to be at odds with received opinion.

In dealing with such cases, a theory which arrives at a sort of 'utilitarianism' by asking the universal-prescriptive question has an advantage over the more standard sorts. It is not difficult to understand why few of us are prepared to prescribe universally that people, and therefore that we ourselves, should be imposed upon, even without our knowledge, in this way. The 'disutility' involved, which escapes the net of utilitarianisms couched in terms of present pleasures or pains, is that of having a desire frustrated which nearly all of us have, namely the desire not to be taken advantage of, even unknown to us. And there are good utilitarian reasons for encouraging people to have this desire.[1]

This manoeuvre enables us to distinguish neatly between two kinds of case which seem superficially similar, but in which we normally give different verdicts. One is the 'electricity' case just mentioned; the other is the case of the person who picks the primroses in the woods, knowing that others will not (because they have no desire to). In both these cases, we are at first inclined to argue that, if everybody acted likewise, the results would be very bad (no electricity for anybody; no primroses; perhaps no woods), and that therefore we cannot prescribe that *anybody* should do it. This seems absurd in the 'primrose' case; and in the 'electricity' case Lyons has shown that the universal prescription, that anybody should use it who knows that the others will not, is not open to the same objection, since everybody's acting on *that* prescription will not lead to a power breakdown. I have already shown why, all the same, we are not prepared to prescribe that people should do this in the 'electricity' case; it remains to notice why the objection

---

1 For a fuller account see 'The Argument from Received Opinion' in my *Essays on Philosophical Method*, pp. 128 ff. and 'Ethical Theory and Utilitarianism' (cited on p. 1 above).

that the desire not to be taken advantage of will be frustrated does not apply in the 'primrose' case. It does not, because only a very few people *want* to pick the primroses; and therefore, if those who do, pick them in moderation, leaving the roots unharmed, those who do not will not feel that they are being taken advantage of, even if it comes to their notice. If a universal desire developed to pick primroses, those who now do it would have a duty to stop unless they could somehow justify the privilege; but, failing such a universal desire, we can readily prescribe that anybody who wants to pick them, and knows that the others do not want to, should pick them.

Applying all this to the case of theft, we see that the thief is asking for a privilege for himself without giving a justification for it. We have seen that if theft became widespread, the institution of property would break down, and have supposed that this would be a sufficiently bad outcome to justify the rejection of the prescription that everybody should steal who wants to. The thief, if he wishes to win the argument, will have to have recourse to the move made by Lyons in the 'electricity' case: he will have to say that it is all right for him to steal, because he knows that not enough other people will do it to lead to a breakdown in the institution of property. But this move we have now shown to be illegitimate; the others all have the desire not to be taken advantage of, and will be taken advantage of if the thief steals while they, out of law-abidingness, do not. They would all like to be able to take other people's property, just as in the 'electricity' example everybody would like to consume more electricity. The 'disutility' inflicted by the thief consists not merely in the harm to the person whose goods he takes, but in the harm to all those who would like to have other people's things, were it legal, but do not take them because it is not, and are therefore taken advantage of by the thief's act. The sum of these 'disutilities' is large enough to make us condemn the thief's act in spite of its utility to him.

If stealing became widespread enough to approach what Lyons calls the 'threshold' (i.e. the point at which any further stealing really would cause the property institution to break down), then the considerations in the 'typhus' example would apply. The 'typhus' example is one in which the threshold has already been reached by even the first man who has lice, if the others have not. The manoeuvre which we have performed in the stealing case was therefore not required in the 'typhus' case, though it would be applicable in that case too.

We have, then, to add the following item to our table of reasons for obeying the law:

C.4   The fact that, if I break the law, I shall be taking advantage of those who keep it out of law-abidingness although they would like to do what it forbids, and thus harming them by frustrating their desire not to be taken advantage of.

The original table was phrased in terms of the 'typhus' example; but since it is obvious how the whole table would have to be generalized to omit specific references to the 'typhus' example, I shall spare the reader this exercise. The result would be a table containing a number of reasons for obeying the law, not all of which will apply in all cases. Our moral obligation to obey the law, therefore, has complex grounds; and I am sure that I have not exhausted their complexity in this paper.

I will end with two questions which have puzzled me. First of all, does the fact that a law is unenforced remove the moral obligation to obey it? We have to distinguish the case in which the law is unenforced but nevertheless generally obeyed out of law-abidingness, from that in which it has become a completely dead letter which makes no difference to anybody's behaviour. In the latter case, reasons C.1, C.2, C.3 and C.4 all go by the board. If the law makes no difference to people's behaviour, the situation in which I am contemplating breaking it is no different in any material respect from what it would be if there were no law; C.1 therefore collapses into B.1. C.2 is obviously inapplicable to an unenforced law. C.3 lapses, because if everybody is already breaking the law when it suits them, their law-abidingness is unlikely to be diminished by seeing *me* also breaking it. C.4 goes because, if breaking of this law is general, nobody is constrained by it to do what he does not want, and nobody, therefore, is taken advantage of if I break it. On the other hand, if the law is unenforced but still widely respected out of law-abidingness, reasons C.1, C.3 and C.4 apply, but not C.2.

The second question is this. Suppose that, in the 'typhus' case, the number of people who delouse themselves when there is a law is identical with those who would have done so had there been no law; and suppose that this is not , as in the previous case, because the law is not enforced (it *is* the case that *if* anybody failed to delouse himself, he would be punished), but because they are all middle-class Americans of cleanly habits and would delouse themselves, law or no law. In that case, by delousing myself I shall be observing the law; but have I any *extra* moral obligation to do this which arises because of the existence of this law? Since other people's behaviour is not affected by the law, the existence of the law has made it no more likely that failure on my part to delouse myself will lead to a typhus epidemic; any increase in the likelihood of this will have been already allowed for under *B.1*, and *C.1* lapses. On the other hand, in this situation reasons *C.2* and *C.3(b)* will remain applicable, but not *C.3(a)* (I shall not be inclining people to break this *particular* law, because they have no disposition to do so). Reason *C.4* will, as it stands, lapse; for if it is not out of law-abidingness that people are doing what the law enjoins, there can be no question of their law-abidingness being taken advantage of. However, the place of *C.4* may be taken by an analogous reason, falling under *B*, if the motive for other people's cleanly behaviour is in part moral: in that case I shall be taking advantage of their good moral behaviour and thus harming them. This presupposes that they have some desire to save themselves the trouble of delousing themselves, but do it from moral scruple. If, on the other hand, their motive is purely prudential, and they have no desire to do what the law forbids (i.e. be lazy and lousy), then the case becomes like the 'primrose' case in this respect, that I should not be taking advantage of them if I failed to delouse myself (though, in contrast to the 'primrose' case, other reasons for conformity would remain).

These complexities could no doubt be extended by asking further questions. But I have perhaps done enough to show that moral reasons can be given, in terms of a formal theory about the logical properties of the moral concepts, for obeying the law in general, and that some but not all of these reasons are weakened or disappear if a law is unenforced but still widely respected, or if it is observed only because people have motives independent of the law for doing what it enjoins. I should go on, as I did in an earlier version of this paper, to ask what are the conditions under which these reasons for obeying the law in general can be defeated by reasons for breaking it in particular cases – the exceptional cases in which there is a moral justification for crimes or acts of rebellion. This question, however, although it yields to the same utilitarian method, must be left for another occasion.[1]

1 I have made a start on it in my paper on terrorism, contributed to a conference on war and violence at Kean College, N.J., to be published in the proceedings, ed. R. Sitelman.

2 Being Free to Speak and Speaking Freely

STEPHEN E. NORRIS

Free speech is among the most cherished of democratic ideas, and in this essay I want to show that it is also very confused. Underlying the confusion are two distinguishable but often undistinguished ideas of free speech, a failure to distinguish sharply between two kinds of risk, and a tendency of discussions of speech to maintain a level of abstraction which diverts attention from important differences among kinds of speech and levels of competence. In combination, these faults lend apparent plausibility to a popular liberal principle which I think deserves to be questioned. I have named that principle 'equal speech,' and I set out its particulars at the beginning of part I of this essay.

One question I wish to raise is whether equal speech can be set upon an Utilitarian foundation. I shall begin by considering a very familiar Utilitarian argument for free speech, and in that context I shall distinguish something I call 'freedom of opinion' from the popular principle I call 'equal speech'. The nature of the distinction will make it clear that the Utilitarian argument at best only supports freedom of opinion, and that it is an argument of the wrong kind to support equal speech.

In part II of this essay, I shall bring the Utilitarian argument for freedom of opinion directly under attack. In this context, I shall examine two crucial premises of that argument: (1) in suppressing an opinion we run the *risk* of suppressing something true; (2) it is undesirable that the truth be suppressed.

Finally, in part III, I shall briefly outline why I think that maintaining a certain level of abstraction lends undeserved plausibility to the principle of equal speech, and why I think that principle needs to be re-evaluated, and perhaps rejected.

I

What I call 'equal speech' is a popular principle according to which two conditions are considered jointly desirable, or even as

13

constituting *rights* of individuals.[1] The two conditions are these: (1) that individuals be at liberty to express their judgments or opinions on matters of concern to them, and especially on matters which they regard as affecting their mutual or separate interests; (2) that this liberty, and the opportunity for its exercise, be distributed more or less equally among individual members of society. The first condition is to be conceived of as being limited by some appropriate principle of harm accompanied by a distinction between 'mere' speech and actions such as inciting, goading, slandering, etc. In other words, the liberty in question is to be regarded as limited in roughly those ways presently accepted by 'liberal' jurists in democratic societies such as England and the United States. When I later talk of 'constraints' and 'restrictions' on speech, I shall mean constraints and restrictions over and above these generally accepted limits on the liberty of speech; and correspondingly, when I speak of 'absence of constraints,' I should be taken to mean all constraints *save* the above-mentioned limits.

The Utilitarian argument I alluded to earlier is the one articulated by J. S. Mill in his essay, 'On Liberty.'[2] There, Mill argues for what I call 'freedom of opinion'. The distinction between this and equal speech will shortly become apparent, as will an ambiguity in the idea of 'free speech' – an ambiguity which invites the mistake of thinking that Mill's arguments can be used to make a case for equal speech. I shall not address the historical question of whether Mill intended his arguments to support what I call equal speech. (However, I think it could be argued that he did not.)

Mill's main thesis concerning 'the liberty of thought and opinion' is this: that whether or not an opinion is in fact true, that it be suppressed would be on the whole undesirable in terms of possible net costs to the community at large. This contention he rests upon what he regards as four distinct considerations. The first is that we are all fallible when it comes to discerning whether or not an opinion is true. Consequently, according to Mill, no matter what the state of one's certainty regarding the worthlessness of some opinion, he will, if he suppresses it, risk the misfortune of having suppressed something true. The second consideration is that

---

1 The concept of a right intended here is that according to which one's having a right to do X involves a correlative obligation on the part of others to forbear interfering. Cf. H. L. A. Hart's discussion of rights in 'Are There Any Natural Rights ?', A. Quinton, ed., *Political Philosophy*, Oxford University Press, 1967, pp. 53–66.

2 Marshall Cohen, ed., *The Philosophy of John Stuart Mill*, New York: Random House (The Modern Library), 1961, pp. 185–319.

because erroneous opinion is seldom enirely that, and because it is only through the collision of such partial errors that what is true in them will precipitate out, suppression again risks loss of the truth, even if the suppressed opinion is in fact erroneous. The third is that the true opinions which we might hold would come to be held 'in the manner of a prejudice' if they were not allowed to be continually and vigorously contested; and so again, we should not seek to suppress opinion adverse to our own. The fourth and final consideration is that even wholly true doctrine, if we are not required to defend it against competing views, will be 'enfeebled, and deprived of its vital effect on the character and conduct . . .'[1]

I cannot say that I find these considerations wholly convincing. They all require the unexamined assumption that it is always a 'cost' to lose the truth, and consequently undesirable ever to risk its loss; and the first of the four considerations would have us believe that suppression always runs this risk. To these points I shall return in sections II and III. About the rest, I shall have little to say. The second consideration, it seems to me, is naively optimistic in the picture it paints of truth, like a fair price, naturally growing out of a free and open market of errors. The third and fourth considerations involve psychological principles about which I hesitate to venture a comment. But let us disregard these possible flaws in Mill's argument.

Let us for the present agree to suppose that all of Mill's points are well taken, and that he has shown what he set out to show. What exactly is it we would thereby have agreed to allow that Mill had shown?

Mill's primary target in the section of 'On Liberty' under consideration, is suppression or inhibition of dissent, whether this suppression be in the form of acts of state, or in the subtler form of social custom and pressure. Dissenting opinion is opinion with a specific kind of content: content which is unwelcome to the 'received' or 'official' view. I emphasize this truism in order to emphasize yet another obvious point, and that is that a dissenting opinion can, given its social and political context, be picked out as such by virtue of its particular content, irrespective of who espouses it, on what basis, or with what special intention or purpose. The importance of this point is that the correlative 'liberty' here is the absence of constraints on the *content* of opinion, and this is quite different from that liberty which consists in the absence of

1 *Ibid.*, pp. 203–46. The direct quotes are from Mill's summary of his own arguments, pp. 245–6.

constraints on *individuals* who might desire to express their views. This difference is often obscured by the fact that, in most actual cases of suppression of dissent, the dissenting opinion is formulated and advanced by specific articulate individuals. Thus, in such cases, whether we describe the situation as one in which a particular *opinion* with a particular *content* has been suppressed, or whether we instead describe it as one in which specific *individuals* have been silenced, we shall in either case have described what is materially the exact same state of affairs. None the less, there remains an important conceptual distinction between constraints on the content of opinion and constraints on individuals. For, it is plainly possible to fix limits on content without at the same time laying down any restrictions as to *who* may offer opinions within those limits; and it is also possible to allow only a privileged few to speak at all, but without restricting the content of what they may say.

That condition of society which consists in the lack of constraints on the content of opinion is what I call 'freedom of opinion,' and it is that condition which Mill's arguments show to be desirable, if they show that much. But to have proved the desirability of this condition, is not to have proved thereby the desirability of there being no restrictions concerning who is to be permitted to voice an opinion. To put the matter vividly: the liberty of every and any opinion to seek advocates does not entail the liberty of every and any individual to speak freely to whatever issue it pleases him at the moment to consider. It is an argument for the latter that equal speech requires, but Mill has supplied us with no more than an argument for the former. It is in this respect that the Utilitarian argument in 'On Liberty' is of the wrong sort to secure the principle of equal speech.

Of course, the variety of constraints one might impose on content are not all of a kind. For example, one professor silences a student because the student espouses views contrary to the professor's teachings; another silences a student because the student argues irrelevantly.[1] Both of these cases involve the imposition of constraints on content, but they each involve the application of very different criteria as to which aspect of content calls for curtailing the act of speech in question, and consequently, we might want to treat these cases differently. Additionally, there are complex cases of the following sort, involving conditional constraints on certain

---

1 I owe this example, as well as my recognition of the flexibility of the idea of suppression 'on the basis of content,' to my colleague, David A. Conway.

individuals with respect to specific kinds of content. We might bar someone from speaking publicly on political issues because he is generally incoherent, the level of confusion being sufficiently high without his contribution. Or, we might forbid someone to publish his views on education while allowing him to continue to teach physics at the university; and we do this because he is intellectually dishonest when discussing matters of the former kind, although scrupulous and forthright when it comes to the latter.

But it is nevertheless important to notice the conceptual distinction between constraints on the content of opinion and constraints on individuals. For, it is important to see that whatever value attaches to the correlative liberty of the one kind does not automatically attach to the liberty corresponding to the other. Gaining sight of this much is essential to putting oneself in a position to see that it is at least consistent with recognizing the value of a high level of intellectual freedom, that we at the same time challenge certain precepts of democratic ideology. The popular principle of equal speech is one such precept that could in this way be consistently challenged, and so too is the romantic notion with which it is often associated: the notion that each individual member of society has his own unique and important contribution to make to the 'pooled intelligence constituted by the contributions of all.'[1] I shall consider the possible grounds for such a challenge in part III. But first I want to examine two important theses involved in the Utilitarian argument for freedom of opinion.

II

Two crucial theses in the Utilitarian argument for freedom of opinion seem to be: (1) whenever we suppress an opinion, we run the risk that we are suppressing something true; (2) it is undesirable that the truth be suppressed (or, it is less desirable than its not being suppressed). The conclusion we are asked to draw is that it is undesirable that any opinion be suppressed, or at least, that freedom of opinion is a more desirable condition of society than a condition in which some opinions are stifled. Recall that Mill bases the first of the two theses on the premise that we are all fallible regarding our judgment of what is true or false; and he even suggests at one point that to seek to suppress an opinion one

---

1 John Dewey, 'Democracy and Educational Administration,' *School and Society*, vol. 45, no. 1162 (April 3, 1937), p. 459.

believes to be false is tantamount to supposing oneself infallible.[1] The second thesis he never explicitly argues for. I shall return to these two theses momentarily.

The conclusion we are asked to draw from (1) and (2) is one which I think those premises cannot generate directly. There seems to be a missing step in going from the relative undesirability of suppressing something which *is* true to the relative undesirability of suppressing an opinion which *might* (for all we can know) be true. The missing step is this: it is (relatively) undesirable to suppress the truth, therefore, it is (relatively) undesirable to *risk* suppressing the truth. I do not find this inference acceptable. But to attempt to show to anyone's satisfaction that it isn't would, I think, require a general discussion of what role, from a logical standpoint, should be accorded to risks in the context of determining preference and choice. This general issue falls beyond the scope of this essay. But I do want to point out at least this much: if the inference in question can legitimately be drawn, this is not so because of its form. The pattern exemplified is roughly this:

X is less desirable than Y;

therefore, risking X is less desirable than risking Y.

There are arguments of this form which are not valid. Relative to having to mind a neighbor's cat for a day or two, most would find it *less* desirable to fall off the face of a cliff and be killed or crippled. But there is nothing inconsistent in the idea that one who had such preferences might yet find it *more* desirable to *risk* falling off a cliff than to *risk* being put in a position where he would be obliged to mind his neighbor's cat, even if we suppose the amount of risk to be the same in both cases. That is, we could well imagine that one who preferred being in the company of a cat to actually *sustaining* serious injury, might yet rather go mountain climbing for the weekend (and hence risk injury), than risk being put in the position of having no excuse to refuse to mind his neighbor's cat. This case suggests a class of slightly different cases, cases of acts of daring, where the desirability of *risking* mishap varies *inversely* with the desirability of actually having the mishap occur. This is not even to mention those cases in which (extrinsic) desirability attaches to risking the undesirable because of the pecuniary rewards of taking the risk in public. I have in mind, here, such

---

1 *The Philosophy of John Stuart Mill*, p. 205. (The discussion which follows should not be misunderstood to be about the *word* 'risk.')

things as being shot out of a cannon, or allowing oneself to be trussed up with chain, boxed, and dumped in a river.

Examples such as the above ought to at least make us pause to consider how it is (*if* it is) that the undesirability of actually suppressing the truth entails the undesirability of risking its suppression. But let us now return to the two theses mentioned at the beginning of this discussion.

Is it true that whenever we suppress an opinion, we run the risk of suppressing something true? This question is not as straightforward as it looks. The risk involved here is an *epistemic* risk, and the persuasiveness of thesis (1) as a premise in the argument for freedom of opinion may turn in part on having us confuse this kind of risk with risks of another kind.

The contrast to which I want to call attention is that between an epistemic risk and what I shall call a *causal* risk. An example will illustrate the distinction. Imagine a political situation in which for us to silence the advocates of a dissenting opinion would be to run the risk of having that opinion become a rallying point, and hence become more popular than it might otherwise have become. We could even say here, that by suppressing the opinion in question we risk *making* it popular. The risk in this example is a *causal* risk; by silencing the advocates of a particular opinion we provide part of the conditions out of which the popularity of that opinion might grow. By way of contrast, we do not usually *make* an opinion *true* by suppressing it, and it is only in special cases that by suppressing an opinion we provide any of the conditions for its truth.[1] Rather, the kind of risk we characteristically take with respect to truth, and the kind of risk I call an *epistemic* risk, is simply the risk of being mistaken in our judgment of whether some opinion is true or false. One runs this sort of risk in suppressing an opinion, only to the extent that one's relevant convictions are subject to error. Specifically, one runs the (epistemic) risk of having suppressed something true just to the extent that he is likely to have erred in having judged the suppressed opinion to be false. The epistemic risk involved in suppressing an opinion one believes to be false thus owes its origin to a possibility of error which would remain even if the suppression had not actually taken place.

The importance of the distinction between epistemic and causal

---

1 The special cases include predictions and threats the fulfillment of which might be provoked or even ensured by attempts to suppress them: e.g., 'The people will overthrow the tyranny of the oppressors,' or better yet, 'The tyrants will try to silence us!'

risks is this. It helps us locate the status of the question: do we risk suppressing something true whenever we suppress an opinion, even when we have the best of grounds for the conviction that it is false? This question turns out to be, at bottom, an epistemological question, and one that could be formulated in a less misleading way, thus: is there, in the case of every one of our judgments, or in the case of every one of our judgments about X matters (factual, political, etc.), the possibility of our being mistaken? Put this way, the question is seen to be one which is not specifically about the wisdom or desirability of suppression. This is not to say that epistemic questions, and the possibility of epistemic failure, are irrelevant to the issue of suppression. But to see that this question is not specific to suppression, is to put oneself in a position to take note of a very important difference in the way in which such epistemic risks, as opposed to genuine causal risks, bear logically on rational choice and preference.

Causal risks, like the risk that by suppressing an opinion we might increase its popularity, are characteristically risks we can (at least in principle, as they say) decide directly to take or not take. We might for example, decide not to run the risk of making our adversary into a martyr by burning him in public. Instead we send him off to Van Diemen's Land, and provide him with all the comforts. But no corresponding option is open to us in connection with the (epistemic) risk that in judging something true or false we might turn out to have been mistaken. If there is this risk inherent in judgment, or in judgment of a specific kind, it clearly is not a risk we can avoid running by taking some alternative action. We can suspend judgment, but that is not an alternative action. The point is even clearer in the context of *beliefs*, for there is not there, as in the case of judgment, the tendency to think that we are always talking about an epistemic 'act' of some kind that we could decide directly to do or not do. Most of our beliefs grow naturally out of the conjunction of our predispositions and perceptions; indeed it is *these* beliefs, and not those which arise when we *venture* a judgment, which constitute the convictions most likely to incline us to suppress the contrary opinions of others; and these beliefs, no less certainly than judgments, are capable of being in error. Plainly, we cannot in the case of these beliefs, do anything directly to avoid the risk of being mistaken.

Noting this difference between causal and epistemic risk alters our estimation of the character and force of the thesis that in stifling an opinion one always runs the risk that the truth is being suppressed. For, there is seen to be a clear sense in which whether or not to run *this* sort of risk is not a question which calls for a *tactical* decision, as is the question of whether to risk making an opinion a rallying point, or whether to risk making martyrs of its advocates. But the persuasiveness of this thesis in the context of the Utilitarian argument for freedom of opinion may turn on its *looking* as if the question *is* one of tactics. The beauty of the Utilitarian argument is that it makes it *look* as if deciding not to suppress a given opinion were a matter of making a rational choice concerning what is the most productive *course of action* given the goal of increasing (or of not decreasing) human knowledge and its benefits. But the way the argument would have things look is precisely the way they cannot be, given that it is an epistemic rather than a causal risk to which we are urged to attend. For, there are no *courses of action* on a par with and alternative to *taking* an epistemic risk. Indeed, such a 'risk' is neither taken nor avoided, but suffered.

But now we must ask whether we suffer this epistemic risk with respect to each and every opinion we might contemplate trying to suppress. If we do not, then it is not clear that in every case of suppression there is the risk that the suppressed opinion is true; and if there is not this risk in every case, then the Utilitarian argument for freedom of opinion is seriously weakened. For it would then have to be allowed that there are cases in which we could *know* that the opinion we contemplate suppressing is false, and *know* that there is no risk of suppressing something which we might later find out was true. The only way to avoid having to allow this, is to maintain the absolute generality of the thesis that we risk suppressing something true *whenever* we suppress an opinion. What I want to suggest is that the required generality cannot be maintained without taking a radically skeptical stance about the possibility of human knowledge, or about the possibility of knowledge in some specific area of discourse, e.g., moral or political discourse. By a 'radically skeptical' stance I mean not the cautious hesitancy which attends ordinary good sense, but rather the view that in the case of *each and every* one of our convictions (or convictions of a specific kind e.g. moral, political) there is a real possibility[1] of our being in that case mistaken. The necessity of

---

[1] I mean to contrast 'real' with 'logical' possibility. To say that in every one of our judgments of, say, matters of fact, there is the *logical* possibility of our being mistaken, is not, as far as I can tell, to say any more than that judgments of fact are contingent, and not logically necessary. It has never been clear to me why holding this position should qualify one as a skeptic.

taking this skeptical stance is shown by the fact that the more modest (and true) position, that human judgment is fallible, is not sufficient to secure the required generality of the thesis that we risk suppressing the truth *whenever* we suppress an opinion. Simply put, to attempt to secure the required generality in this way is to commit the fallacy of division.

To say that judgment is fallible, if it is to take a position short of radical skepticism, is simply to say that we and the world are so constituted that we can err. The evidence for this is undeniably clear: a substantial number of our judgments do turn out to be in error. But while it might follow from our general fallibility that the chances are that a *substantial number* of our future judgments will be in error, this neither means nor implies that in the case of each judgment there is a *substantial chance* of its being in error. To argue that this is implied, is to endorse the pattern exemplified by the clearly fallacious argument: a *substantial number* of students in this class will fail the exam, therefore, each student in this class has a *substantial chance* of failing the exam.

That a skeptical stance is required to secure the generality of the thesis that we risk error in every case in which we might seek to suppress an opinion, is not necessarily an indictment of that thesis. One might, after all, find skepticism unobjectionable. But that skepticism is required in this context gives some urgency to the question of whether, indeed, it is a tenable position, and if it is not, whether freedom of opinion can be set on some other foundation. I shall not attempt to answer these questions here, except to emphasize the point that the fallibility of human judgment does not imply radical skepticism. The question remains as to what does imply it.

Much of the force of the preceding argument depends on construing the risk involved in suppressing an opinion as being, at bottom, an epistemic risk. But there is a challenge to this way of construing the matter, and it is this. There is a positive connection between truth and benefit, and the presence of this connection lends support to the view that there is genuinely a causal risk involved in suppressing an opinion. That some truth might not come to light, might well result in the loss of some benefit which would have been derived from the knowledge of it. If this, then the risk in suppressing an opinion would seem not to collapse to the possibility that we might be mistaken in judging it false. Super-added, there would be the risk of losing some concrete benefit. This risk seems to be of just the right kind to play a legitimate role in the framework of decision. It is a risk about which we can ask, 'Shall we or shall we not take it?', for it is a risk which we can reasonably seek to avoid by direct action or forebearance. In short, it seems very much to be a causal risk. Does this challenge vindicate the thesis which has been brought under attack in this discussion? Not really. Two points need to be made in this connection.

First, we face the risk of losing access to some benefit of knowledge only in those cases where the opinion we contemplate suppressing either is true, or might be true, for all we can know. The causal risk of loss of benefit thus hinges on the epistemic risk that we might be mistaken in having judged the opinion in question to be false. But we are now brought full circle to ask, again, whether this epistemic risk is present in every case. The question poses the same dilemma as before: there is this risk in every case only if radical skepticism is true; and if there is not this risk in every case, then there are cases in which we could know that we are not suppressing the truth, and hence know that we are not risking the loss of any benefit knowledge of the truth might give us.

Second, to suppose that the risk of losing some benefit attends every case of suppression of what *is* true, is at least to suppose that knowledge of the truth is always beneficial. In essence, it is to endorse the second of the two theses cited at the beginning of this discussion: (2) It is undesirable that the truth be suppressed (or, it is less desirable than its not being suppressed). But it is far from clear that with respect to every conceivable truth, general knowledge of it would be more desirable or beneficial than ignorance. Suppose, for example, that it is true, as some writers have recently maintained,[1] that there is a scientific basis for the view that American Negroes as a group are intellectually inferior to American Caucasians as a group. Is it so clear that in a society where racist sentiment is yet strong, the publication (and hence general knowledge) of such a thesis would be either beneficial or desirable? I shall not say that such a view clearly ought to be suppressed, but at the same time I wish to press the question whether it is so evidently clear that it ought *not* be suppressed. It is irrelevant to this question whether or not any racist principles logically follow from the alleged scientific fact of intellectual differences between

1 I am referring primarily to an article by Arthur Jensen entitled 'How Much Can We Boost IQ and Scholastic Achievement?', in *Harvard Educational Review*, Reprint Series No. 2 (1969). But also see R. Herrnstein, 'IQ,' *Atlantic Monthly* (September 1971).

whites and blacks. For, as any student of history knows, what a thesis logically implies is hardly an accurate measure of the effects it will have on the behavior of those who find it attractive; and this is especially so when we have good reason to think that many who would find it attractive would care more for its abuse than for its logical consequences.

With these remarks I quit the discussion of freedom of opinion. I hardly think that anything I have said here justifies abandoning that principle. But I do think I have shown the need for a re-examination of its scope and foundation. I now want to redirect our attention to equal speech. For here is a principle I think we may be better off without.

III

Just as nothing said so far justifies abandoning the principle of freedom of opinion, nothing said so far shows that the principle of equal speech is without foundation. What has been shown is that equal speech cannot rest on a certain kind of argument for freedom of opinion, both for the reason that the former principle is distinct from and not entailed by the latter, and for the reason that the argument for the latter that we have considered stands in need of revision, if it can be salvaged at all. The viability of the principle of equal speech thus remains a question unanswered. I shall not attempt to answer that question here. But I do want to offer several brief remarks concerning the kinds of issues an attempt to answer that question must confront.

Concerning the viability of equal speech, two sorts of argument in defense of that principle suggest themselves: one advanced from the standpoint of the society in general; and the other from the standpoint of the individual. According to the one argument, each individual's opinion on matters of general concern is supposed to have some intrinsic worth, and consequently, it would risk loss of some benefit to society to silence any individual who wished to express his views on such matters. According to the other, each individual has a right to participate in political decision-making processes because his interests are affected by the outcome of those decisions.[1] The former sort of argument suffers all the ills which beset the previously discussed thesis that suppression risks

1 Dewey seems to hold both of these positions. See note, p. 17.

loss of the truth. But in addition, both sorts of argument appear to me to require for their cogency, the maintenance of a certain level of abstraction – a level of abstraction which is quite out of place given the practical import of the principle of equal speech. I give this challenge substance by posing the following questions.

First, there is the question of whether the phrase 'matters of general concern' really denotes a genuine category or *kind* of concern – that is, whether it names a homogeneous body of concerns, each one like another in that they all require us to bring to bear essentially the *same* level of competence in the application of essentially the *same* kind of knowledge. It is not obvious how one would argue for an affirmative answer to this question, and consequently, it is not obvious how one is to maintain the general position that *each* individual's opinion on *any* matter 'of general concern' has some intrinsic worth.

Second, there seem to be two kinds of interest which must be separately considered in determining what, if any, individual rights grow from the fact that decisions of governments affect individual interests. On the one hand, it may be in one's interest that a decision fall to this rather than that side of a clear-cut issue: that, for example, a bridge be built here rather than there, because the former location would directly benefit one's community, or oneself in particular. On the other hand, it may be in one's interest that a decision be made in accordance with certain standards: that, for example, the bridge be built *well* regardless of where it is built, and that it be built well for the least cost. In the case of the first sort of interest, it is by no means axiomatic that one's interest should be allowed to compete with others just because it is someone's interest. One's interest can, after all, be illegitimate from a moral or legal standpoint, in which case one would not be entitled to pursue it, vocally or otherwise. In the cases of the second kind, where it is in one's interest that certain standards be met, it is not always in one's interest to be a participant in the decision-making process. There are many cases where to have the one interest is in fact not to have the other. For example, if one possesses no more than a layman's knowledge of bridge design and construction, then it is clearly not in his interest to have decisions pertaining to such matters influenced by his (ignorant) opinions, even though it might be in his interest that a particular bridge be built well. Similarly, a person's interest in remaining generally healthy does not, if he has no special knowledge, generate an interest in being party to decisions as to which food additives should be allowed to remain on the market.[1] To the contrary, it is in his interest that someone better qualified than, and hence other than himself, be party to those decisions.

The importance of the above examples and of the distinctions they illustrate is this. How well a bridge is built and which food additives are allowed to remain on the market quite easily qualify as 'matters of general concern;' but they are also matters which require the competent application of different sorts of knowledge. Thus they illustrate how the ruberic 'matters of general concern' obscures the heterogeneity of the class it designates. In much the same way, the level of abstraction at which discussions of the rights of free expression and participation are often carried on, obscures the same heterogeneity. The result is that it is made to look as if the majority of social and political issues are such that good will and the proper application of ordinary common sense are sufficient for their correct disposition. Or, alternatively, one is led to think that except for a few special cases, there is no literal sense to be given to the idea that one answer to a social or political question could be more or less correct than any other. It is not clear that either of these alternatives accurately pictures the majority of social, economic and political problems faced by twentieth-century industrialized societies. The first must be regarded as presenting a wholly false picture of things unless we are willing to stretch the idea of common sense beyond recognition. The solution of contemporary problems will require the application of a variety of special skills, among them the ability to tell sound from fallacious reasoning – an ability not yet generally recognized as one among other *technical* skills. As to the second alternative, it would seem that some form of skepticism or subjectivism is necessary for its defense. But it should not at this point be a surprising hypothesis that liberalism requires such foundations.

Moreover, the distinctions among the kinds of interest one might have regarding decisions which affect him, press the question of *which* sort of interest it is which generates rights with respect to speech and participation. Here again, maintaining a certain level of abstraction allows one to say, with some apparent plausibility, that rights of speech and participation grow out of one's interest in the outcome of the decisions of one's government. But which interest is it that generates these rights? Is it the interest one might have in

---

1 Although, it might generate an interest in influencing the selection of those who will make such decisions.

one of several possible outcomes of a deliberation? Is it one's interest in having certain standards met? What rights should we suppose to be generated in the multitude of cases where it is in no one's interest, or in the interest of only a few, that decision be left to the haphazard divinations of incompetence?

The acceptability of the principle of equal speech hinges on how we answer these and related questions. Specifically, there is the question of whether we are willing to trade off competent political participation in return for the value of relatively unfettered freedom of advocacy. It needs to be re-examined, first of all, whether the latter is rightly valued. But this re-examination must be carried out in the context of a carefully constructed system of categories of speech, which takes into account such things as the kinds of subject, circumstance and function of speech. For I think it will become evident, once considered, that it is neither just nor productive of any benefit to treat each instance of speech like every other. Putting forth an idea, without argument or evidence, may be a legitimate way of initiating productive discussion among one's professional colleagues, or among one's students. But advocating a policy which is likely to affect the lives of millions is quite a different matter. The first is experimental or exploratory speech, while the second calls for action on the basis of the position advocated. That they are both instances of speech, seems hardly a sufficient reason to insist that they be subject to the same constraints, or absence of constraints. Again, to publish or broadcast an interview with a coal miner on the subject of working conditions in the mines, seems to me a legitimate way of providing a large number of people access to a first-hand description of those conditions. But to publicize the same miner's opinions on foreign policy is quite another matter. He might, on the one hand, be a man who is well informed on the subject, and just happens also to be a miner. But on the other hand, he might instead be a miner who just happens to have a few unexamined and uninformed opinions which he is quite willing to share. That these cases are all instances of speech, is no reason to treat them alike.

The general category of 'speech', or even of 'political speech', must give way to the results of a more refined analysis if we are to enable ourselves to adopt the frame of mind necessary for considering the possible benefits of abandoning the principle of equal speech. As things stand, the mere thought of constraints beyond the ones presently imposed in democratic societies raises the spectre of the slippery slope implicit in the question. 'Where do we draw the line?' The reply is that there in not one but many lines to be drawn, and the accelerating degeneration in the quality of political discourse in 'free' societies is motivation enough to begin to carefully consider where they should be drawn.

3 Respect for Persons and Social Protest

EDWARD KENT

This essay is addressed to what is felt to be the single most important problem facing contemporary societies, namely that of identifying and securing the well-being of persons. The social ideal set forth, respect for persons, serves as a device for focusing attention on certain guidelines for reform in both social theory and practice. The analysis begins with four preliminaries, then briefly elucidates the ideal of respect for persons, next criticizes authoritarian elements endemic in modern communities, and finally makes an appeal for the further development of new subsidiary identity-groups which press their interests and concerns through active protest.

Four preliminaries

In her influential article, 'The Language of Political Theory,' presented to the Aristotelian Society more than two decades ago,[1] Margaret MacDonald directed an attack against the whole enterprise of political theory, its upshots, and its irrelevancy to the way governments actually perform and to the concrete problems with which they wrestle. Her arguments mirrored Karl Marx's challenges to ruling-class ideologies, but were equally critical of institutionalized Marxism. If the constructs of Hobbes, Locke, Rousseau, Kant, Hegel, Bentham, Mill and others, as some had argued, were no more than veiled justifications of capitalist self-interest, Marx's own corrective speculations had spawned Stalinism, a bureaucratic authoritarianism equally oppressive towards individuals' interests and to the quality of life lived by the supposed beneficiaries of a new social and economic order.

---

1 Read as a paper to the Aristotelian Society 1940-1; reprinted in A. G. N. Flew (ed.), *Essays in Logic and Language*, Oxford, 1951.

Abstract political models

These are as likely as not to distort the political reality which they are designed to clarify, and they are subject to exploitation by unscrupulous political leadership. The 'law and order' implications of Machiavelli's doctrine of the prince and Hobbes's doctrine of the absolute sovereign haunt us to this day. Locke's natural right to private property has corrupted American economic practice since it was first preached from New England pulpits in justification of the American Revolution. The lands of the Indians were expropriated because they did not 'mix their labor with the soil'; corporate enterprise has exercised license against the public interest in the name of 'private' ownership; intelligent control of resources has been virtually impossible in the United States because private property is enshrined in the Constitution. Rousseau's General Will gave rise to the Reign of Terror and continuing instabilities in the French political structure. Hegel's ethic of the absolute state offers a continuing challenge to individual liberties and the claims of private conscience. Classical natural-law theory and liberalism generally have generated inertial factionalism in the face of the large issues of this century – war and the control of economic resources.

Miss MacDonald is persuasive in claiming that something in the very conceptual structure of political theorization is flawed. Manifestly political theorists are bound into their own cultures, yet they claim to speak with absolute authority and for all times. They attempt to identify constants presumed to give universal validity to what are in fact time-bound speculations. Human nature, for instance, is conceived as impermeable – or else subject to refashioning according to specifiable causal laws. History is taken to evolve under guiding universal laws (divine, scientific, economic, psychological or whatever). Rational consensus is said to demand that men pursue goals X, Y, Z and abide by rules of conduct Q, R, S. Yet even if some constants can be identified, are they an adequate foundation for a complete and enriched political system? When one examines this or that formulation, a pattern of rationalization usually emerges. A claim is staked for one or more first principles of right thinking or right action, perhaps a set of natural rights, a conception of justice, or an ultimate ideal. Subsequent elaboration inevitably calls for qualification of the preliminary postulates to bring them into accord with practical realities. Qualification in turn opens the floodgates of factional interpretation, as when

Catholic natural-law theorists divide over private property or the just war. Or, the basic norms are found to be defeasible. John Rawls's *A Theory of Justice*[1] can be read as a sustained refutation of its own first principle, equal liberty.

Despite their conceptual weaknesses traditional political theories nevertheless live on in the public consciousness as low-grade ideologies and slogans which all too frequently take the place of reasoned persuasion in the formation of public policies. Wars are always just, the other side the aggressor. Political leaders cloak their schemes under an umbrella of concepts stripped of specific meaning – 'freedom,' 'democracy,' 'justice.' Above all else, traditional ideas of all ideological persuasions are wielded in defense of established authority. A significant political phenomenon of this century has been the frequent diversion of attention of political leaders from the traditional enemies without to something else, to which we now turn.

The enemy within: the place of dissent

Almost imperceptibly, the era of the Cold War, which pitted nations and ideological blocks against each other, has been overshadowed by the phenomenon of dissent arising within systems. Russian hegemony over Eastern Europe was threatened during the 1950s by a wave of revolts by striking workers and dissident political officials. The People's Republic of China next experienced its own internal upheavals. The Western democracies in turn erupted with student and worker protests while détente between East and West was in its preliminary stages. And as the détente reached its climax the Nixon administration turned its attention to the 'enemy within' – students, progressives, dissident minorities, members of the opposition parties. Central to each of these revolts has been the threat or actual use of violence.

Traditional political theories have left little alternative but to interpret them as revolutionary. The strong doctrine of sovereignty enshrined in Western political theory makes little or no provision for challenges to established authority which move outside conventional legal channels. Mill's admonitions regarding the potential tyranny of even democratically elected majorities have not until very recently engendered any corresponding theoretical provision for selective political dissent.

1 Oxford, 1972

Even recent restricting criteria for defining civil disobedience – behavior which is non-violent, public, conscientious, selective, involving a willingness to accept arrest and punishment – are inadequate. New terms such as 'resistance' and 'civil refusal' have been generated to fill the gaps in the full spectrum of living social protest. Yet what Gidon Gottlieb calls 'veto communities' are still struggling to establish the legitimacy of their resistance to felt tyrannies in all types of political regimes.[1] The absence of theoretical support for legitimate protest movements throughout the world is a sad commentary upon an almost instinctive tendency to sustain legitimate authority in all its excesses from the Holocaust to the wars in South East Asia.

One-dimensional analysis

One cannot but be struck in surveying the academic scene with the limited awareness of our current social problems within the perspectives of separate disciplines. Political scientists and economists tend to dominate foreign policy to the exclusion of culture-oriented specialists. Here there is the scale-map approach to South East Asia which produced the American fiasco. In the United States, particularly, piecemeal solutions to problems have created administrative chaos in the lives of average citizens. Housing policies are generated independently of welfare, welfare administrations are oblivious to the safeguards of due process, highway programs are imposed with scant attention to ecological or demographic consequences. Profit-oriented corporate giants run roughshod over public interests. Even the physical sciences function in disarray. Biochemists warn of potentially disastrous consequences of excessive use of fertilizers and unstable new plant strains while agronomists press on in fanatical pursuit of maximum food production – the so-called Green Revolution. In the United States the term 'planning' is held suspect because of socialistic connotations.

Complex problems

The very complexity of the social, economic, and political prob-

1 Gidon Gottlieb, in Eugene V. Rostow (ed.), *Is Law Dead?*, New York, 1971.

lems confronting theoretical analysis comes close to making the enterprise itself a doubtful one. At the very least theorists must continually retool conceptually, be attentive to new factual and theoretical data which challenge their cherished assumptions. Philosophers particularly are guilty in this regard. Too frequently they fall back upon revised versions of traditional intellectual systems which have already proved unworkable. They resist the implications of new data – if they are willing to accept factual data into their world-view at all. Quite absurd proposals continue to emerge from the philosophic community. A return to moral anarchism is urged – I will only do what my conscience tells me to do, and expect others to do likewise – but no account of existing power-realities and how to deal with them is forthcoming. Systems-analysis is urged as the solution to all human problems – what is good enough for a battleship is good enough for human society – with no recognition of the authoritarian implications of systems-analysis. The Establishment is identified as the enemy, which may be true, but the identification provides only a starting-point for comprehensive social analysis.

The easy ideological or theoretical solutions offered for our contemporary problems do not help with the greatest of what might be called the practical ones. Can food or energy production keep up with our practical requirements? Will pollution or an ecology crisis bury us all in the end? Can mass societies (or their leadership) retain their collective sanity in the face of overwhelming new challenges? Any of these questions presents a potentially radical challenge to our conventional moral and legal assumptions. We are living in a century of 'final solutions' (some already attempted) which defy the imagination. A civilization which has optimistically assumed for many centuries that future problems are amenable to human solution may have to face up to the terrifying prospect that some vital ones are not. At the very least it may be necessary to convince ourselves in the interest of future generations that a radical reordering of our priorities is called for, for example, a shift from military defense to conservation of limited vital resources as our highest practical aim. Long-standing attitudes and habits of response may check and delay crucial decisions beyond a point of no return.

Its past and recent history, then, displays both dangers and great shortcomings of political theory. In what follows, although I shall not mention them again explicitly, I shall have both in mind. I shall propose, as I have said, an ideal of political behavior which recurs to the person in the process of decision-making and suggests a search for new vehicles of expression for individual claims and demands.

Respect for persons

The ideal of respect for persons is firmly embedded in the Western religious and legal traditions. It is ambiguous, entailing various notions of worth, moral agency, and special rights and duties, all of which generate complexities. Kant brought the concept into philosophic prominence, welding together religious, moral and legal senses of respect for persons in his writings in diverse areas. He identified the worth of persons with the good will, thus abandoning previous external ranking systems – standards of wealth, power, birth, role in society, intelligence or whatever which had tended to dominate religious as well as secular culture. Kant distinguished between claims of moral agency which require that persons be treated as 'ends and not means solely' and the less rigorous legal-political standard of a natural right to equal liberty. His analysis has endured in the face of major competitors – utilitarianism, Marxism *et al*. Rawls's *A Theory of Justice* builds upon the Kantian corpus with its implicit criticisms of utilitarian and Marxist formulas for subordination of individual interests to the welfare of the whole.

This analysis of respect for persons departs at significant points both from Kant and contemporary extensions of his position. Kant's conception of persons was notoriously moralistic and assumed a degree of freedom of the will which few could accept fully today. His harsh doctrine on criminal offenders, for example, while representing a gain in historical context, is now generally held to be offensive. Extreme punishment and perhaps even the distribution of wealth according to moral merit are implicit in Kant. His account of rationality was narrow in its implications for a definition of personhood. Criminals, the legally insane, and others who one way or another offend against a sense of justice or propriety, are only constructively claimed as persons. They are objects to be punished or treated, entities whose rights have been forfeited.

The present analysis, in contrast, considers as candidates for personhood all those who articulate claims and demands, as well as those (e.g. fetuses, mental defectives, future generations) whose claims are voiced by other agents. This elucidation leaves some shadows in penumbral areas – should 'human vegetables' be sustained by advanced medical techniques? – but its paradigm instance of personhood is clear: the individual who enunciates claims and demands. Under this conception the psychopath (whom Stanley Benn[1] reads out of his canon) and others remain as persons.

The conception also involves objection to John Rawls's elaboration of the primary good of self-respect, central to justice as fairness but incompatible with my own sense of justice as respect for persons. Rawls maintains:

> Perhaps the most important primary good is that of self-respect . . . . We may define self-respect (or self-esteem) as having two aspects. First of all . . . it includes a person's sense of his own value, his secure conviction that his conception of his good, his life plan, is worth carrying out. And second, self-respect implies a confidence in one's ability, so far as it is within one's power, to fulfil one's intentions (*A Theory of Justice*, p. 440).

My first disagreement lies with Rawls's identification of self-respect with self-esteem. Self-esteem is clearly a valuational term referring to one's sense of one's own worth. Self-respect may also be used to refer to worth. However, it has a second function, performative rather than valuational, captured in various dictionary senses of the term 'respect.' To respect is 'to regard, consider, take into account, to pay attention to, to observe carefully.' This second sense of respect is in a fundamental way value-free – free particularly of the various worth-grading systems of contemporary societies (moral worth, economic or social status, intelligence, performance, loyalty to party or regime, and so on). It has a function somewhat analogous to legal due process, which insists on certain safeguards for defendants (right to written charges, legal counsel, cross-examination of witnesses, etc.). The ideal of respect for persons similarly insists that the claims of persons, regardless of their status, be granted a fair hearing – be considered, taken into account, paid attention to, observed carefully, etc. By further implication, the standing of the claims and demands of the individual should not be made contingent upon his 'sense of his own value, his secure conviction that his conception of the good,

1 Stanley I. Benn, 'The Ideal of Community', read as a paper to Philosophy and Public Affairs, New York Chapter, November 2, 1972.

his life plan, is worth carrying out.' Rawls's notion of respect is too narrowly associated with a perfectionist ethic, 'a rational plan of life and in particular one that satisfies the Aristotelian Principle' (ibid., p. 440). 'Rational' is the slippery word here. The Aristotelian Principle (enjoying one's realized capacities) is at once too binding and too vacuous. There are too many life-styles and human practices which are debatably 'natural' (the older term usually associated with the Aristotelian ethic). They include homosexuality, religious asceticism, military combat, saintliness and heroism. Individuals with rational life plans are favored in Rawls's broad outline of justice, but is this distribution inherently fair?

Again, Rawls's identification of self-respect with self-esteem leads him to take as merely support for self-respect what is here viewed as a necessary condition. According to Rawls, 'finding our person and deeds appreciated and confirmed by others who are likewise esteemed and their association enjoyed ... [is a] ... support [for] the first aspect of self-esteem, the sense of our own worth.' Certainly this is a psychological truth – our sense of our own worth is reflected back to us by others. However, respect for persons focuses on a second and very different kind of practical truth – we feel that our claims and demands are being attended to (respected) when they are in fact granted public consideration. There is no requirement here that persons granted public respect be esteemed nor that their claims and demands be vindicated. Presumably if the said claims are defeated after being given consideration, reasons should be offered for their denial – excuses or justifications. (This consideration cannot be elaborated here.) There is, indeed, considerable evidence that social protestors who demand respect neither expect esteem from established authorities nor anticipate satisfaction of their demands. Black protest literature in the United States demonstrates a steady progression from an esteem- to a respect-oriented platform. Notice the sequence in the following book titles: *The Invisible Man* (Ralph Ellison), *Nobody Knows My Name* (James Baldwin), *Why We Can't Wait* (Martin Luther King, Jr), *Seize the Time* (Bobby Seale), *Blood in My Eye* (George Jackson). The increasing stridency of the demands of oppressed groups is a world-wide phenomenon. Violence or the threat of violence is only the ultimate in attention-getting devices.

The ideal of respect for persons does not detail which claims and demands are to be vindicated. It does suggest that political vehicles for response to all articulated claims and demands had better be devised if we are to sustain the democratic ideal. In the next section of this essay authoritarian instrumentalities which threaten this ideal in political systems of all ideological persuasions will be examined. It will be argued that we must at least begin by attending to the voices of oppressed persons and groups before we can hope to effect the compromises and the winnowing-out of vital from non-essential interests which lie at the heart of the democratic enterprise. A climate of respect for the special interests of others is essential to our shared well-being. Violence, criminal or revolutionary, is the obvious concomitant of our lack of respect for strongly felt claims and demands.

Authoritarian instrumentalities

Despite the existence of democratic ideals, the practical exigencies of decision-making processes in liberal as well as socialist regimes betray authoritarian strains which threaten respect for persons. A list of democratic ideals can be contrasted with authoritarian instrumentalities.

Democratic ideals	Authoritarian instrumentalities
Popular participation	Managerial efficiency
Equality	Élitism
Persuasion	Propaganda
Communication	Manipulation
Co-operation	Coercion

The proper balance between ideals and instrumentalities has always been a delicate business in political theory. In his *Republic* Plato limited the range of application of what are called democratic ideals to his guardian élite. Aristotle granted full political participation to citizens only. The religious tradition of the West, under the influence of Roman Law and natural-law theory, has been basically authoritarian. Machiavelli romanticized the more manipulative instrumentalities of authoritarianism. Hobbes attempted to subvert an emerging democratic ideology with his powerful doctrine of absolute sovereignty. Locke accentuated managerial efficiency as his primary citizen virtue (a precedent written into the American Constitution). Marx and Mill favored an élitism which still dominates socialist and liberal political practice. Manipulation of popular opinion, which up to World War II was supposedly permissible only in authoritarian systems, has been made respectable by political scientists in the liberal democracies.

There seems to be a direct line of devolution of authoritarian instrumentalities from the relatively innocent appeal for managerial efficiency to the obvious villainies at the bottom of the list. Bureaucracies once established, democratic or communist, develop interests of their own. When persuasion fails to move recalcitrant masses, propaganda and manipulation are the natural recourses for getting things done. If all else fails, coercion is a last resort. Plato's fundamental criticism of democracy, that the clash of competing claims and demands generates instabilities which in turn encourage a demagogic coup, has been vindicated time and time again in this century. The competition to increase gross national products during the latter half of the century carried the seeds of recourse to expertise (élitism) for getting things done, resort to propaganda and manipulation characteristic of government policies in this decade, and finally the threat of coercion. It should be no surprise that the American War on Poverty was displaced by wars against the enemies without – and within.

The striking feature of authoritarian instrumentalities is that they cut across ideological lines and hence suggest weaknesses endemic in the very structures of contemporary social organization. Marx's willingness to defer 'participatory democracy' until the millenium and his call for the dictatorship of the proletariat made quite explicit the authoritarianism of state socialism. Less apparent was the ongoing struggle against authoritarian movements built into the fabric of social and liberal democracies. Only the strength of particular democratic cultural traditions seems to have preserved democracy as a political institutuion. Possibly only by accident of religious tradition have a few countries avoided at least an occasional lapse into dictatorial rule during this century. This paper makes no special brief for any particular religious tradition but does note in passing that only nations with a strong history of tolerance for religious dissent seem able to resist authoritarian impulses in times of national crisis.

Extending this analysis of the authoritarian syndrome further, one might expect its manifestations to emerge in those groups favored with special powers or privileges – especially in the domain of economic controls. If one identifies power-groups narrowly as those which control the means of economic production – managers of state enterprises in socialist regimes and private capitalists in liberal ones – the pattern does seem to have been followed frequently in the developed industrial communities. A more fluid situation seems to obtain in Third World countries where indigenous economic power groups are not so fully evolved. 'Popular' leaders rather than economic interests stand a chance of capturing the public imagination and in consequence the political decision-making process. Since these leaders owe their power to people rather than economic power groups, they seem more responsive to the popular will. Certainly in both East and West, military-industrial complexes have first call on economic resources. So-called 'countervailing forces' have been powerless to check these juggernauts.

Liberals have been peculiarly reluctant to accept the implications of economic power for political rights. Theorists have resisted the notion of the 'sovereignty of private property,' the direct correlation between negative and positive freedoms. The legal community, which deals with the daily workings of economic power, has not been overly communicative in detailing the special privileges of wealth before the law and the special deprivations of poverty. Socialists for their part have viewed nationalization of wealth as a panacea for all social ills without recognizing that state managers can be as ruthless and indifferent to individual claims and demands as private ones. The locus of power may vary from one system to another but the temptations of the authoritarian instrumentalities seem common to all. Popular participation, equal consideration, rational decision procedures are repeated casualties of authoritarian ideological cover-ups.

Particularly in the domain of administrative law the most fundamental safeguards of due process are disregarded. A new generation of American poverty lawyers has been fighting to restore – despite considerable official resistance – some safeguards in a wide range of areas that affect the poor: public housing, welfare rights, medical services. But vast administrative areas – regulatory agencies, public utilities and service agencies – still bring to bear with relative impunity the full force of bureaucratic mindlessness if not outright favoritism towards vested interests. The individual is subject to pressures and controls more reminiscent of the feudal estate than anything corresponding to the ideals of modern democracy. Petty tyranny of public and private organizations strikes virtually every household at one time or another. And if ordinary agencies impose in petty ways upon everyman, special institutions – prisons, mental hospitals, the military – are modern reflections of long-forgotten hells. The most fundamental human rights are abrogated at whim even in the most humane systems, and there are few to which the term *humane* can be applied. The effects of ordinary institutions – schools, medical facilities, police, welfare – upon the urban poor, are growing more barbaric in the United States where authoritarian solutions are increasingly announced as public policy. Law and order, benign neglect, black capitalism, national security, work ethic, and other smoke-screen slogans disguise manipulation and raw coercion. This attitude even attacks democracy itself as a conception of the good society. The Nixon administration, with the support of powerful economic interests, attempted to take over the agencies and institutional safeguards of American democracy. This was an offshoot of classical liberalism, or of liberalism's capacity for allowing special interests to grow powerful and to dominate the political process.

Neither liberalism nor socialism have found ways to check the pressures of authoritarian instrumentalities confronting democratic ideals.

Identity groups and social protest

The twentieth-century experience should have made it apparent by now that mass democracy is not the universal social panacea it was once conceived to be. It patently cannot survive periods of crisis in national systems in which democratic ideals are not already deeply embedded. Under the best of circumstances, 'tyranny of the majority' threatens weaker interest-groups. Election to political office and the distribution of resources are constantly subject to manipulation by power groups. Specialization, the isolation of expert knowledge, and ever more complex practical problems further compromise a decision-making process designed to accommodate the common-sense preferences and deliberations of the average citizen. A widening credibility gap between national leadership and the voting populace – a crisis in confidence – is an almost predictable outcome of the structure of modern democracies apart from the covert manipulations of this or that administrative or legislative body. It is not surprising that studies of American group attitudes in the early 1970s found that every significant ethnic, regional or occupational group considered itself to be a minority under siege by outside forces beyond its control. Endemic paranoia is an expectable consequence of the feelings of powerlessness that individuals and groups experience in the tidal flow of contemporary decision-making processes. We are all in a sense refugees from each other in the give-and-take of the political and economic market place. Only the least informed still find a comfortable identification between self and nation which seemed to be the inevitable trend of the nationalism of the first half of the century. We now hold suspect our own national leadership as much as, if not more than, our conventional enemies of a few decades past.

More and more, it seems, individuals are groping to find their identities in smaller group allegiances – allegiances to an ethnic group, an old or a newly instituted religion or political party, a professional or occupational organization, a community association, a collection of friends, a leisure-time activity with like-minded individuals, and, despite severe critiques of it, the nuclear family. Particularly in the United States new interest groups are formed overnight which bind together complete strangers in fervently shared commitments and activities.

There is also the world-wide tendency of student generations not to pledge allegiance to older and traditional organizations but rather to institute their own associations, formal or informal, overt or covert. Greater proportions of individuals than ever before have the opportunity in three or four short years to alter completely their aspirations, sense of reality, life-styles. Such extensive change is bound to generate great anxiety for all involved – the past generation, those left out of this novel formative experience who have already joined the work force, and those who find the transition a wrenching experience in its own right.

The radical divisions in contemporary societies between attitudinal groups thus separately formed by their cultural experiences are only surprising in that more violent conflicts than have already transpired have not erupted between new and old believers. National political campaigns during the late 1960s and 1970s have seen radical readjustments along precisely the political lines one would expect from this analysis. Will the polarization continue as more individuals become self-conscious in their respective identity groups?

The danger inherent in this situation is that demagogic appeals rather than true group interests may determine elections (or governmental coups) and thus national and domestic policies. In the immediate future one anticipates a power struggle between sharply divided majorities/minorities with winner-take-all stakes. Left or Right dictatorships may attempt to impose their single solutions through the manipulation of state power. The majority of the world's population already lives under such controls. Under such conditions protest and resistance will have to take new forms. Even where formal democracy endures, however, authoritarian tendencies will have to be resisted in new ways in measure with the threat of a final plunge into the fully manipulated authoritarian state from which there is no easy return.

It is fortunately true that concurrently with the emergence of the new authoritarian instrumentalities, methods of resistance short of full-scale revolution have been pioneered and tested. They can be utilized to curb both petty and grand tyrannies. As noted earlier, it is possible to assemble groups with common concerns and to mobilize them into effective protest communities on short notice and with relatively limited resources. Using sophisticated devices, small groups can bring to bear power greatly out of proportion to their size. A number of techniques – some new and others modifications of old practices – have been utilized effectively.

(1) *Publicity*   Mass communications media make possible widespread publication of claims and demands, at least when effective techniques are utilized for drawing public attention. Choice of an attention-getting tactic is of greater importance than is generally recognized in the shaping of public opinion or the curbing of excesses of authorities. The use of violence by initiators of change, for instance, is a particularly dangerous tactic, one which can boomerang and induce counter-resistance in the public mind and support for official oppression. Civil disobedients, Gandhi and Martin Luther King, Jr, were quite aware that violence or evidence of oppression must be clearly attributed to opponents, lest the disobedients achieve at best only a moral stand-off position in the public consciousness. The practice of civil disobedience in the Soviet Union, where protestors are subject to continuous official oppression, has become a fine art practiced with extraordinary effect given the circumstances. Ridicule, official embarrassment, threats to official vital interests (e.g. trade agreements) have proven far more effective protest instruments than more traditional violent methods (bombing, assassination) still used elsewhere. The appropriateness of the publicized act to the situation protested seems of paramount importance in achieving protestant aims.

(2) *Legal resistance*   Many more legal recourses for resistance are available to protestors than readily meet the unprofessional eye.

Sometimes large numbers of concerned individuals can bring to bear pressures not available to the isolated person. Large groups can with effect disrupt vital social functions by blocking modes of transportation, refusing to pay taxes, refusing to carry out military orders. Selective boycotts can influence corporate policies in certain industries and smaller community contexts. The Nixon administration claimed that it had been continually sabotaged by revelations of official policies by holdover workers of previous administrations. The Watergate lesson should not be lost on protestors in democratic regimes – the truth is still a powerful weapon. Specific legal remedies may be discovered in the existing body of law (e.g. heavy fines paid to individuals for evidence of industrial pollution) or may be introduced by concerted lobbying efforts (e.g. increased fines or criminal sanctions for such things as consumer fraud, anti-trust violation, housing violations, etc.). Groups willing to focus time and energies on a single issue carry power beyond their mere numbers when their efforts are concentrated on all possible means of redress (viz. Ralph Nader).

(3) *Illegal resistance* When officials are unwilling to enforce existing laws or when legal means of redress are inadequate, further steps can be taken which cross the line of legality but which still maintain effectiveness. Civil disobedience, illegal strikes, disobedience of restrictive court injunctions, have all made their impact in recent decades. Illegal disruptions can force issues upon the public's attention through the arrest and attendant publicity of criminal trials of resistors. Here again the greater the sophistication and ingenuity of the protestant devices, the greater their effect.

(4) *Violence* Violence deserves special attention as a resistance device. It is an old instrument associated with revolution and may in all but the most extreme contexts be as outdated a tool as revolution itself. Driven to counter-violence, all but the most shaky modern political regimes will win the violence-game. As Lenin noted in a much-quoted passage, with the invention of the machine gun violent revolutions in well-established states became a thing of the past. Even Hitler came to power by legal means. Only where a relative balance of power exists may violence be expected to redound to the favor of (slightly) weaker powers. (They may be better mobilized or have some other special advantage, such as world opinion, on their side.) The use of violence may salve outraged senses of injustice but it does not automatically

stimulate reforms – or if so, only at the cost of too much human suffering. The use of violence requires extreme justifications which are only sometimes available.

Turning from the tactics of resistance to the alternative strategies which theorists have proposed for groups subject to felt injustices, critical attention must be directed to proposals of several contemporary schools of thought.

Many, influenced by the traditional models of state sovereignty and authority, have been reluctant to acknowledge the right and obligation of suppressed groups to resist oppression outside conventional legal channels. John Rawls, for instance, reluctantly sanctions the right of civil disobedience against violations of the equal liberty principle but looks askance at protests directed against injustices in the distribution of social and economic resources. He has had nothing to say about the inequitable practices of the criminal justice system. Rawls's model of society is still pervaded by the social atomism of earlier social contract theory: allocation of resources by legitimate authority to individuals conceived as quantifiable economic units. The model has no conception of social interest groups, the special powers and disabilities, say, of corporate wealth *vis-à-vis* the ghetto community.

The new anarchism of Robert Wolff (*In Defense of Anarchism* and 'On Violence')[1] and others also focuses upon the individual to the neglect of sub-communities. Appalled by abuses of official authority, Wolff calls for the restoration of individual conscience as guide to action. There is a partial truth involved in this position: many of the excesses of the twentieth century have come about because individual conscience has capitulated to official command – one recalls the notorious war criminal defense of Eichmann and his predecessors at Nuremburg. But moral anarchism offers no solution to the problem of coercive powers, which are an inescapable feature of modern societies and also a necessary instrument for the preservation of justice.

An alternative formulation of the power-problem seeks a middle ground between fealty to absolute state authority and moral individualism. In a series of essays (*Obligations: Essays on Disobedience, War and Citizenship*)[2] Michael Walzer has expounded a notion of obligation to identity groups which supersedes

1 Robert Paul Wolff, 'On Violence,' *Journal of Philosophy*, vol. 56, no. 19, October 2, 1969; *In Defense of Anarchism*, New York, 1970.
2 Michael Walzer, *Obligations: Essays on Disobedience, War and Citizenship*, Cambridge, Mass., 1970.

national loyalties. Alienated and oppressed groups will transfer responsibility from the state to particular interest group. Gidon Gottlieb ('Is Law Dead?' and 'Toward International Consensus')[1] has introduced the concept of 'veto communities' and a consensual model of law as a counter to the traditional coercive-hierarchical model of classical sovereignty theory. Working from separate academic disciplines but with close attention to current events as well as theoretical schemata, Walzer and Gottlieb have attempted to project new courses for political protest. The return to the middle ground of liberal pragmatism seems common to many radical commentators of the late 1960s.

The notion of divided loyalties has been anathema since Hobbes framed his model of indivisible sovereignty. The dissenting tradition has always been a minority current barely sustained by religious sects and groups – Quakers and others – who have objected strenuously to sovereign commands which abrogated conscience. Only in this century has conscientious objection been considered tentatively as a 'right', and it is far from being established as that. Political idealists are generally held suspect, out of touch with practical realities. Books are written which argue that dissidents really suffer from psychoanalytic disorders, are immature or at best inexperienced. But such reductivist treatments seem blind to the fact that previous generations have never been so fully exposed by the educational process – both its formal aspects and the dramatic exposures of the mass media – to the realities of the contemporary world and particularly to the injustices inflicted upon segments of population. Simplistic ideological explanations no longer satisfy. It seems inevitable that to an increasing extent individuals will choose deliberately both their affiliations and their primary loyalties and responsibilities.

This is to be explained in good part by the extraordinary increase in dissemination of information about the real workings of social institutions. Also, contemporary intellectual systems generally concur one way or another in holding individuals responsible for that of which they are (or should be) aware. Given Sartre's account of false consciousness, the psychoanalytic exposure of motives, the Marxist critiques of the gap between the appearance of society and the real substructures, and simply reasoned analysis,

---

1 Gidon Gottlieb, 'The Nature of International Law: Toward a Second Concept of Law', in Cyril E. Black and Richard A. Falk (eds), *The Future of the International Legal Order*, vol. 4, *The Structure of the International Environment*, Princeton, 1972, pp. 331-83.

individuals and groups can no longer claim innocence of the serious flaws in the social and economic fabric. Rigorous excuses and justifications can be and are demanded for social policies. The attitude 'my country, right or wrong' can no longer prevail. Even the institution of law has been deprived of sanctity and is now viewed as a very rough tool for achieving at best only proximate justice.

Loyalty once attached to traditional institutions is redirected to persons or association groups which win personal attachment and commitment. With the breakdown of the 'habit of obedience', new centers of obligation and commitment arise to sustain the identity of the individual. Anomie is an intolerable state for most individuals to endure for any significant period of time.

One of the special assets of the urban environment has been that so many option groups are available to suit almost any individual set of proclivities. For every dehumanizing social agency there can spring up some sub- or counter-cultural group in which the individual can find himself attended to and respected as a person. The peculiar vitality of fringe religious sects can only be understood in terms of their contributory role in the lives of otherwise lost or unnoticed persons. Extremist political groups in many cases play similar roles. The individual seeking respect for his person will find it where he can.

Certainly identity groups may be dangerous to individuals and may not represent their best interests. Caution, however, must be exercised in such a judgment. Individuals may join political and other organizations which are exploitative, but one must take seriously their need to associate themselves with power figures, ego-ideals, or sometimes simply those with whom they feel comfortable or those who share their attitudes and concerns. The underlying reasons why individuals do not choose identity groups which best represent them must always be paid attention in the truly democratic society. Reformers, for example, may put off potential followers by patent arrogance and élitism. Lack of respect for persons – finding them not as they are but rather as it is thought they should be – is a prime sin of reform movements. The challenge is to bring into being coincidence between identity and interest associations.

The special value of identity groups in relation to social protest is that they serve as centers of power subsidiary to the governmental structure. The primary flaw in most contemporary democracies has not been that there have been too many lobby groups but rather that there have been too few representing too narrow a spectrum of interests. The history of labor movements is evidence of what can be done in the course of time to fulfil the needs of weaker parties. The struggle to win recognition and legitimacy by labor was bloody and violent. But labor is now so firmly established in most industrial societies that it in turn can afford to play the role of oppressor of still weaker groups which it excludes from its hard-won benefits. There is scarcely an interest group so puny that it cannot mobilize support for its interests if it is well led and organized. Smaller groups benefit from their smallness in that their over-all demands are relatively slight in cost to the body politic. Larger ones can bring considerable pressure to bear on the public mechanisms of government given the narrow balance of power in many electoral situations.

The tools of protest which have been developed in recent decades have proven to be powerful ones, and as newly-emergent groups become more sophisticated in the use of these tools they should increase their impact significantly on the formation of social policies. A few hundred German wives managed to deter the Nazis from deporting their Jewish husbands to concentration camps by the expedient of a public demonstration. Contemporary governments are not always the invincible juggernauts that many conceive them to be. They can be vulnerable when pressures are applied at the right points with finesse, timing, and determined intent. Even authoritarians are sensitive to public opinion if no other court of appeal is available. Exposure of the secrets of the tyrant can be more injurious to his authority than acts of violence directed at his regime.

In sum, if modern societies confront the individual with a massive array of potentially repressive instrumentalities, persons may nevertheless discover powerful weapons in the arsenal of social protest. Persons, speaking and acting out their concerns, are their own best defense against large- and small-scale tyrannies.

4 'Bad Day at Big Rock': The Assessment of Political Confrontations

L. J. MACFARLANE

Politics has two closely associated dimensions – assessment and action. The most chairbound political philosopher is usually concerned to persuade others as to the validity of his theoretical position, the most impatient and unpredictable activist will normally have some prior aim in view. Men move rapidly from one dimension to the other, and in fast-changing situations need to do so if they are not to be overtaken by the very events they would control. In any political situation we have persons making political assessments and acting on the basis of these assessments, and the assessments and actions of others are part of what is assessed, acted on and reassessed as the situation develops. ' What is happening' always appears as what is 'seen' to be happening by some particular person or persons, who 'interpret' these events for themselves and others in their own terms. The shape that interpretation takes will turn on the relationship between what these terms are and the nature of the developing situation itself.

All political events emerge within an existing political system, out of prior political situations and problems, and against a chaotic background of often conflicting political forces, values and influences. Men make of this welter what they can and what they will, despite the fact that neither ability nor purpose are fixed or independent resources at a man's discretionary disposal, but potentials within a distinctive changing social context. Nevertheless the practical upshot is that each of us has a set of values and beliefs, of varying degrees of comprehensiveness and unity, which we hold to as our own. In consequence we are rarely, if ever, confronted by political crises which leave us completely disorientated. We make sense, that is, of the present unexpected or uncongenial turn of events in terms of the conceptions and approaches we have already arrived at. Similarly we appraise others' reports of current events in terms of these same conceptions, discounting some and marking up others. However, the actual turn of events, especially where it assumes a highly unexpected or injurious form, will have its own direct impact on the continuing assessment we make of the

48

situation in question. It may indeed even lead to a reappraisal or rejection of our fundamental conceptions and values.

In this essay[1] an attempt will be made to show the interconnection between values, events and assessments by constructing an artificial confrontation situation, but where the ingredients are drawn closely from the stark reality of the United States negro problem. In this way it is possible to construct a model which can be used to illustrate certain hypotheses about the nature of the process of political assessment. At the same time by staying sufficiently close to reality, a check can be kept on the analysis by noting the kind of reactions different people have made in very similar live positions. It is perhaps worth making clear that the model here displayed is one which has been devised in the course of exploring the confrontation exercise discussed below. It has been tested and revised in the process of exploration. What is presented, therefore, is a run-through of the final version – not an account of the problems one faces in trying to devise and test a model of this sort. Confrontation situations, while not typical of politics, highlight the underlying principles and approaches which move men to think and act politically, and enable one to distinguish more clearly between the various ingredients involved in political assessment. The sharpest confrontations which arise are those between the organs of the state and a political party or movement. At the extreme the confrontation assumes the form of a struggle to overthrow the state or to smash the political party or movement. Since, however, with the doubtful exception of the May 1968 events in France, no such situation has arisen in Western states for the past forty years, I have constructed my conformation at a less fundamental level, while introducing revolutionary elements into the scene.

In Big Rock, a small Southern town in the United States in the middle 1960s, there exists a local Civil Rights group consisting of members of different civil rights organizations and of individuals, which has been campaigning for some time for ending racial discrimination. It has had some small success in securing the

1 The ideas developed in this paper have their origins in two earlier writings of mine: 'Justifying Political Disobedience', *Ethics* (Chicago), vol. 79, no. 1, October 1968 and *Violence and the State*, ch. 8, 'Force and Violence' (T. Nelson & Sons, 1974). The dramatic heading 'Bad Day at Big Rock' comes from the marriage of the old film title 'Bad Day at Black Rock' with the southern township of Little Rock, scene of the famous *Civil Rights* disturbance. The paper has benefited from discussion at the Social and Political Study Group at Oxford University.

abandonment of segregation in parks and libraries, but has been unable to secure any concessions in the fields of education and housing from the public authorities. Its leaders have, therefore, announced a protest march through the town and called on all negroes and their white supporters to join in. The local elected white police chief bans the march and an appeal by the Civil Rights leaders to the elected magistrate to have the ban rescinded fails. The leaders announce that the march will go ahead as planned along a route leading from an assembly point just outside the town boundary. The police chief issues a public warning that the police will stop the projected illegal march at the point of entry to the town. The Civil Rights group issues leaflets calling for full negro support for the march, but instructing participants not to use violence or resist arrest and to obey all instructions from march marshals. 'If we aren't allowed to pass, there will be a mass sit-down.' The small but active Black Power group within the Civil Rights Movement issue their own broadsheet which urges 'don't sit, keep marching and fight back', and gives advice on 'how to protect yourself from white pigs – what to wear and what to carry'.

On the day of the march the police assemble just inside the town. They are led by the Police Chief, a southerner bitterly opposed to racial desegregation and convinced that negro opposition can only be overcome by superior force. He is accompanied by his younger Deputy, who is also opposed to desegregation, but who believes that the movement towards it cannot be stopped but only slowed down. Since the official climate of federal opinion is against segregation, it is important to avoid confrontation situations which might force federal intervention. He draws a clear distinction between a show of force as a deterrent and the use of force, except in situations which can be made to seem defensive.

In the front ranks of the police are two officers A and B. A is a liberal-minded officer, rather out of favour with his fellows, because he accepts the principle of ending racial segregation and has strict views about the use of force by police officers. B, on the other hand, is a strong believer in the use of force to uphold the authority of the police and to keep the blacks in their place.

Leading the demonstration is the Rev. W., the dominant figure in the local Civil Rights Movement. He is an alert politician who has become dissatisfied with the uncompromising moral position of Gandhian non-violence to change the hearts of one's opponents. He now thinks in terms of using moral and political pressure to force concessions from the authorities. He recognizes, however, the overriding need to hold together the varied elements in the Civil Rights Movement and the dangers of losing out to the growing Black Power Movement. Behind and near him are three demonstrators – X, a black moderate, member of the Southern Christian Leadership Conference and a staunch adherent of Gandhian non-violence; Y, a powerful black student civil rights militant, and a member of the Congress of Racial Equality who supports direct political action as the only alternative to physical violence; and Z, a member of the local Black Power group.

At the side of the road just in front of the police are a group of spectators, including P, Q, R and S. P is an apathetic white who happens to be passing. He would prefer to keep things as they are, but is not prepared to act to defend the status quo since he does not believe that any alteration is likely to affect him adversely to any major extent. Q is an elderly black defeatist who would like to see a change in the position of negroes but who sees little prospect of any major improvement and believes more harm than good is lilely to come from trying to force the issue. R is a white liberal who strongly supports the Civil Rights Movement but is apprehensive of the growth of militancy and extremism within its ranks. Lastly there is S, a very odd character. S is a Martian philosopher exiled to the United States for un-Martian activities (evidencing signs of emotion and feelings). Although he is white at present he is liable, like poor John Rawls's faceless man,[1] to be made to assume a black form, or suffer impairment of faculties and abilities if the Martian leaders so determine. He is, moreover, sentenced to live for at least one hundred years on earth. It is through the eyes of all these persons that we shall analyse the events of that historic 'Bad Day at Big Rock'.[2]

It has been claimed above that particular political assessments are made in terms of the values and conceptions which people already have about the nature of the political process. In a confrontation

1 John Rawls's conception of justice as fairness proceeds from an intitial hypothetical situation in which the principles of justice are agreed upon by men none of whom know what their place will be in the society they are creating, nor what natural assets and abilities they will possess. See John Rawls's *A Theory of Justice* (Clarendon Press, Oxford, 1972), pt I, ch. 1, s. 3 'The Main Idea of the Theory of Justice'.
2 I have tried to make my 'projections' of the assessments of the characters involved as consistant as possible with their basic positions. I would not seek to argue, however, that only the assessments given are consistent with these positions. The assessments given are to be read as those which characters like X and Y *might well* take up, not necessarily would take up.

situation this prior conception will be revealed in the attitudes taken up towards the opposing forces *in advance of* the particular alignments made and tactics pursued. Both participants and observers of 'Bad Day at Big Rock' will have views about the 'authority' of the bodies involved in the clash prior to its taking place, views about the right of such bodies to act in particular ways for certain specified purposes. It is hoped that by starting from the way in which different men judge whether those in positions of authority (positions which permit or enable them to issue orders or take action on behalf of others) are entitled to act, and for what purposes and in what ways, some light may be shed on the nature of authority itself. The concept of authority will be approached in this essay not in terms of how men use the term authority, but in terms of how they react towards those claiming to exercise different claimed forms of authority. Of course, the former may well affect and be affected by the latter.

Although bodies have existed and do exist which claim an unqualified right to universal compliance with any and every wish or command, for most associations there are implicitly understood or practical restrictions on the actual claims that are made, as well as degrees of non-acceptance and non-conformity on the part of those addressed. The actions of those claiming authority are judged with respect to the fields of operation within which the actions fall. It is thus possible to reject a claim to authority on the score that the claimed field is an inappropriate one for action, either at all or by the particular body concerned. In the case of official authorities, agencies of the state, their field of operation is normally defined by constitution, legal enactment, convention and custom, but inevitably there exists considerable discretion in interpreting these limiting factors and in applying them to particular situations. The urgency of the problem, the extent to which those concerned feel themselves responsible for its solution, the degree of discretion and initiative they believe themselves to have, will all affect their appraisal of what sort of problem it is that faces them.

An official may be involved in a situation in many different ways. At one extreme he may find himself caught up in a problem of neither his making nor expectation, forced to act quickly on his own initiative, without reference to superiors, where existing guide-lines and past experience are of little or no relevance. At the other extreme he may be given specific orders to act in a manner which admits of no discretion and where the only choice is between compliance or refusal to act. In the former situation the official may be held responsible for his actions in a much wider and deeper sense than in the latter. There, the issue of responsibility is focused on his decision to act in that way, rather than on responsibility for the form of the act itself. Even when it is deemed that some person or body has authority to issue orders within a particular field, the specific order may be subject to qualified approval or rejection by reference to the purpose (stated or understood), the method (its effectiveness and validity), the expected consequences (immediate and long term), and, after the event, by the actual consequences. A person who feels doubts on all of these scores may nevertheless carry out his orders because he feels that his position requires it. On the other hand he may fully identify himself with the order in all its aspects. The former person may well sympathize with those against whom he feels constrained to act. The latter is unlikely to do so, although the more farsighted and imaginative may be able to see grounds for his opponents' point of view.

The authority of the police in any local community may be judged by reference to a range of criteria relating to the nature of police responsibility within the political system, their reliability and conscientiousness as servants of the public, and their right to issue orders and to use coercion. While the police perform a wide range of functions those most relevant to the confrontation situation we are dealing with are the maintenance of law and order under the constitution, the enforcement of the law and the carrying out of court orders. In each instance it is possible to distinguish between whether the function is accepted as a valid and necessary police function, and whether the police force in Big Rock are held to be carrying out the function effectively and fairly. In these terms, although only the revolutionary Black Power demonstrator, Z, may be expected to explicitly dispute the validity of these police functions, some of the other negroes may find it difficult to distinguish between law and order maintenance and enforcement, as general functions, and their own experience of such functions at work in Big Rock and other areas. The difference between Z and X, a civil rights moderate, turn less on their basic attitudes to the police law-enforcement function than on their appraisal of what would be necessary to ensure that the function is carried out fairly. The latter believes in the prospect of a progressive movement towards justice between races within United States society, the former sees no such prospect until black revolutionary power reigns supreme.

Amongst the whites outward agreement on police functions masks differences in root appraisals of the nature of American society. Policeman B, the white extremist, sees law and order as a function requiring to be enforced particularly against negroes to uphold and preserve the racial superiority of white power. R, the white liberal, thinks in terms of the strict application of objective laws in an impartial manner, thereby opening the way to the gradual dying-away of racial discrimination. There are also subtler differences between 'the realists' and 'idealists' on both sides; between those who like X and R look forward to the possibility, however distant, of a society in which men may live in harmony one with another, with only vestigial police powers required, and those like the Deputy Police Chief and Q the black defeatist who see men, both black and white, in essentially Hobbesian terms – ever ready to profit at their neighbours' expense.

The underlying conflicts of approach are well brought out with reference to the police responsibility to carry out court orders and decisions, since the courts in the United States, and especially the Federal Supreme Court, are at the centre of the civil rights and racial discrimination controversy. The Police Chief would not accept the implications of the judgment of Supreme Court Justice Douglas in *Garner* v. *Louisiana* (368US. 157, 1961), that 'the police are supposed to be on the side of the Constitution, not on the side of discrimination' and that police action in pursuance of state law or practice upholding discrimination was itself unconstitutional.[1] He sees himself as having a responsibility to his white electors in Big Rock, not to politically suspect Justices of the Supreme Court in Washington. Civil Rights supporters, on the other hand, regard the issue of enforcing Supreme Court decisions as crucial, precisely because in the current context these lend support to the civil rights cause – in contrast to the decisions of the Court in the *Civil Rights Cases* (1883) when it placed a very conservative interpretation on the racial equality provisions of the Fourteenth Amendment of the U.S. Constitution (ratified in 1869), and on the specific power of Congress to enforce these provisions by appropriate legislation.[2]

1 Joseph Tussman (ed.), *The Supreme Court on Racial Discrimination* (Oxford University Press, New York, 1963), p. 114.
2 Richard M. Johnson has shown, however, that although only one quarter of respondents in Eastville, Tennessee, said they personally agreed with the Supreme Court's decision in the *Schempp* case (which forbade religious practices in public schools), and 70 per cent felt that the Court had exceeded its powers, 55 per cent nevertheless acknowledged the necessity

These differences of approach appear even more sharply when one projects views on the fairness with which the police in Big Rock carry out law and order functions as between whites and blacks. While the Police Chief and his Deputy publicly insist that the police act impartially and fairly as between persons of different races, in private they accept that police action in this area is directed to upholding existing discrimination. All other listed persons either accept and assert openly that the law and order function is not carried out fairly between races, or define and interpret fairness in terms of racial inequality (as with Policeman B). Apart from him, and the apathetic 'Don't know' white P, all the listed members of the public, together with Policeman A, agree that the law ought to be carried out fairly and impartially as between whites and blacks. The question of effectiveness presents more difficulties as it is not clearly apparent, even for those in charge, what criteria and standards to use. Since, however, the general level of crime in this small city is low, contrasting favourably with the lurid accounts of big city crime displayed on press and television, and since there have been no racial disturbances to date, the general view is a positive one. However, the Deputy Chief has some misgivings about the upward trend in crime figures in the town and about the lower figures for other towns of comparable size. For their part the Civil Rights supporters, and especially the militants, view police effectiveness mainly from the angle of maintaining racial discrimination. On this issue the Martian philosopher joins the apathetic white P as a 'Don't know' as he finds it impossible to determine to what extent crime levels are a reflection of police activity in any particular locality.

The question of the conscientiousness of the police can be viewed under three headings – corruption, helping the public, and upholding the rights of citizens. On corruption (bribe-taking, using official position or opportunities to further private ends, etc.) while everyone agrees that ideally there ought to be none in the police force, all the police officers feel that some level of corruption is inevitable in the police-world as it is. Police officer B defends the practices he indulges in of taking 'dropsey' from prostitutes, purveyors of pornography and gambling establishments, and assumes that those higher up get larger shares of more lucrative 'perks'. This is indeed true of the Police Chief, but the Deputy has clean hands and, like Police Officer A, is disturbed at the present high level of corruption. The members of the public are also divided into those, like the white Liberal R and the Civil Rights moderate X, who believe corruption might be eliminated or at least sharply reduced in a reformed and more humane society; those, like the Black Power member Z, who see police corruption as but a particular expression of general white rottenness only removable by revolutionary ruthlessness; and those, like the black defeatist Q and P the apathetic white, who believe that corruptness like the poor will always be with us. Everyone, officers and public alike, believes that corruptness is widespread within the Big Rock police.

On the scores of 'upholding the rights of citizens' and 'helping the public' there is acceptance of these by both police and public as roles the police should fulfil, although the black militants Y and Z do not accept that they can be fulfilled within existing white-dominated society. On their side the Police Chief and his Deputy have doubts about citizens' rights. The Chief interprets upholding rights as meaning that the police should determine what rights should be upheld and how. His Deputy does not feel it is possible to combine the fight against crime and the maintenance of law and order with the strict upholding of all legal rights of citizens, bearing in mind the conditions in which the police are operating and the general standard of police personnel. In judging how the police fulfil these duties people are moved mainly by their racial position in Big Rock, but also partly by their particular experience. Even Z has to admit that Police Officer B is very helpful to negro mothers and their babies in the streets. In general, however, the profile of the police appears as corrupt, little concerned with upholding rights, helpful to the middle class rather than the poor, to children rather than adults.[1]

An important aspect of authority is the claimed right to issue orders. In the case of an official body like the police this has both an internal and external dimension. The right of those *in* authority within the force to issue orders to their subordinates is not disputed by anyone – difficulties are liable to arise only with reference to the scope and limits of the authority claimed and the actual orders

1 This profile is taken largely from William A. Westley, *Violence and the Police: A Sociological Study of Law, Custom and Morality*, ch. 3, 'The Public as Enemy', (Massachusetts Institute of Technology 1971).

given. A quite sharp distinction is drawn by police officers between carrying out general rules and orders, i.e. not to smoke on duty and the specific instructions given to a particular officer by a senior officer. The right to issue the former type of instruction is not disputed, but compliance is not necessarily readily given or even widely expected by superiors. In the latter on-the-spot situations, compliance is almost universally expected and received, even where the recipient may doubt not simply the 'rightness' or appropriateness of the order for the situation in hand, but even the 'right' of the superior concerned to issue such an order. Police Officer A, for example, might doubt whether the Police Chief had a right to arrest a passive bystander to the confrontation proceedings, but he would not dispute his Chief's right to order him to effect such an arrest. Acceptance of the right to issue orders is perhaps the most important aspect of any formal authority structure.

More complex considerations arise, when one turns to the claimed right of the police to give orders to members of the public. Here, under normal conditions, one is not dealing with general orders emanating from the central police authority, but with particular officers ordering specific persons to act in a certain way. Individual police officers are not accepted by the public generally as having a right to have their orders obeyed without reference to the content of the order concerned. 'Move along please', or 'Stop singing' are quite likely to evoke an unfavourable response from those to whom they are directed; while those asked to answer questions, produce papers or have their person or baggage examined may not only refuse, but may specifically deny the right of the police to give such orders. At a different level many persons, on varying grounds of self-interest or personal inclination, are likely to refuse or fail to go to the aid of a policeman when he calls for help in carrying out his duties, especially if such assistance involves the risk of injury from assailants.

The attitude of the Chief of Police and Police Officer B are that the public ought to carry out all commands given to them by a police officer, the former accepting that the validity of the order might be raised with a superior officer after the event. This is to apply the command procedure used within authoritarian bodies like the army and police force to those outside the force. The Deputy Chief of Police is much more aware of the need both to keep order-giving to the minimum and to approach members of the public in a conciliatory rather than an aggressive manner. He is less concerned, however, than Police Officer A with orders being lawful and reasonable than with their not creating difficulties. Amongst the civilians the Black Power supporter Z, and to a large extent the young militant Y, do not accept that white 'pigs' have any right to give orders to blacks, nor do they accept that blacks have any obligation to obey such orders, although they may of course decide to do so for their own reasons. The apathetic white P, and the black defeatist Q, see no point of talking in terms of police rights – all that counts is whether the police have the power to enforce compliance and this will depend on the situation concerned. The Civil Rights leader, the Rev. W, and the moderate X together with the white liberal R and the Martian philosopher S, accept that in order to carry out their proper functions the police need to have both the right to give orders to members of the public and the right to call on them for support. They emphasize, however, that in the longer run compliance, especially in situations where the police need assistance, will turn far more on the extent to which the police are accepted as playing a helpful positive role within the community, than on the claimed extent of police authority to command or its capacity to require conformity to orders.

These varying attitudes towards the authority of the police to act come into sharp focus over the issue of the right to use coercion. While only Z, the Black Power militant, rejects the right of the police to retaliate against those who attack them, where the attackers are negroes, not only Y, the young militant, but the Civil Rights leader, Rev. W, the moderate X and the white liberal R, do not accept that the police have an unconditional right to use force against those resisting arrest. They have seen or heard of too many situations in which police officers have attempted to arrest negroes without, in their view, due cause. In such cases Y claims that the victims have a right to resist arrest and ought to do so, the Rev. W sees a right which ought not to be exercised, and X neither right nor obligation to resist. Nor do these five accept the unqualified right of the police to use coercion against those disturbing the peace or breaking the law, with the police the sole judges of when the peace and law have been broken and of the need to use force (and the form and degree required) to remedy the situation.

While our Martian philosopher sympathizes with this position he points out that since the police are the main body on the ground responsible for maintaining peace and enforcing law, only they can possibly determine whether force is necessary. They may make mistakes (indeed some mistakes are inevitable), but that cannot be a reason for denying them the right to use coercion. This means relying on their judgment of when coercion is justified and required. On the other hand there is hard evidence of the inequitable use of coercion against negroes in Big Rock which suggests to S, in his vulnerable position as an outward-human liable to a colour transformation, the need to attempt not so much a restriction of police powers but a change in composition and attitudes, especially at the top. These views find some echo in Police Officer A who, while asserting the authority of the police to use coercion in carrying out their functions, believes that the emphasis should be on the use of minimum coercion required to secure strict conformity with the law. He would himself feel required, however, to carry out an order to use force against a person which he thought unjustified, except in the most extreme circumstances i.e. against defenceless women or children. No such inhibitions move his colleagues, who in their varying ways and with differing sensitivities are only concerned with the impact of the use of violence, not its validity.

If we now turn to the specific confrontation designed for the unfortunate inhabitants of Big Rock this will first be analysed from the police angle in terms of police aims and objectives, the methods proposed to realize these objectives, their advance assessment of consequences, immediate and longer-term, and their assessments after the event. The stated well-publicized objective of the Police Chief is to prevent an illegal (i.e. banned) march taking place, but there is a widely rumoured and accurate belief that the actual police objective is to teach the negroes in Big Rock a lesson, i.e. learn it doesn't pay to challenge white authority in the town. The rumoured objective *r.o.* goes beyond the stated objective *s.o.* but is not inconsistent with it. For most persons *r.o.* incorporates *s.o.* The attitudes towards these objectives are as shown in Table 4.1 (below), where everyone believes that the police objective is in face *s.o.* plus *r.o.*

The inclusion of the Martian philosopher S in the second column arises from his view that once the relevant authority (in this case the local magistrate) has upheld the ban on the march, the police have a legal responsibility to stop the march taking place – the *s.o.* follows logically from the magistrate's decision, having regard to the role of the police in the United States system of government.

As the Rev. W orders the Civil Rights marchers to halt some thirty feet in front of the ranks of policemen armed with riot shields, batons and C.S. gas rifles, the Police Chief takes up a powerful loud-speaker hailer and orders the marchers to disperse peacefully. 'I'll wait ten minutes and if you haven't moved by then my men will move in to clear the streets. You are breaking the law. Go home or take the consequences.' Everyone accepts that the

Table 4.1 Police objectives

endorse *s.o.* endorse *r.o.*	endorse *s.o.* reject *r.o.*	reject *s.o.* reject *r.o.*
Police Chief Deputy Police Chief Police Officer B apathetic white P	Police Officer A Martian philosopher S	Rev. W moderate X militant Y Black Power Z white liberal R black defeatist Q

course of action proposed by the Police Chief will enable him to secure his stated objective of stopping the march and dispersing the marchers. Opinions differ sharply, however, on whether they will secure or assist the realization of the rumoured objective of teaching the negroes not to challenge white authority in Big Rock, thereby securing a sharp reduction in the level of Civil Rights activity in the town.

Table 4.2 Assessment of effectiveness of proposed police action against marchers in relation to level of Civil Rights (C.R.) activity

Reduction in C.R. activity	Increase in C.R. activity	Don't know
	Deputy Police Chief Rev. W	
Police Chief Police Officer A	moderate X militant Y	apathetic white P Martian philosopher S
Police Officer B black defeatist Q	Black Power Z white liberal R	

The question of the legitimacy of the methods proposed by the police to secure both stated and rumoured objectives is more difficult to handle. This is so since aside from certain forms of political action, such as torture or indiscriminate terror, which may be indefensible in all conceivable circumstances, political means cannot be properly considered apart from the ends they serve. That is not to say that they cannot be considered apart from the legitimacy of the ends. It is possible to assert, as does the Geneva convention, that the use of tanks in warfare is not illegitimate and the use of poison gas illegitimate, without determining whether war in general or any particular war can be or is justified.

Table 4.3 Assessment of validity of proposed police action against marchers to secure police objectives

| Stated objective | | Rumoured objective | |
Action justified	Action not justified	Action justified	Action not justified
			Officer A
Police Chief (PC)	Rev. W	PC	W
Deputy Chief (DPC)	moderate X	DPC	X
Police Officer A	militant Y	B	Y
Police Officer B	Black Power Z	P	Z
apathetic white P	black defeatist Q		Q
	white liberal R		R
	philosopher S		S

It is not easy, however, for those involved in a particular confrontation situation, like the Big Rock incident, to separate off the validity of the methods proposed from their assessment of the validity of the ends these methods are designed to serve. In this context the notion of validity is expressed in terms of assent to the proposition that the police would be justified in using the means proposed to secure their stated and rumoured objectives.

While the Martian philosopher S endorses the stated police objective he cannot accept the validity of the action proposed to secure it. He feels that although force may well be necessary to disperse the marchers, the Police Chief is not making any efforts to negotiate with the Civil Rights leaders to secure a peaceful compromise, e.g. permitting a limited number of representative marchers through to see the Mayor or allowing them to sit down on the side of the road, leaving space for traffic to pass. Police Officer

A shares some of these presentiments but is more inclined to hold that, having stated that the marchers will be dispersed, the police will have to disperse them, especially since there are elements in the march concerned to make the confrontation a trial of strength and authority. He no more than S, however, can accept the use of force to teach the negroes of Big Rock a lesson. The Deputy Police Chief agrees that the police will be justified in acting as proposed to disperse the marchers to secure either the stated or rumoured objective but he argues that they would be unwise to do so, at least until they have put on a public show of willingness to negotiate with the Civil Rights leaders. Such negotiations may take any form providing that the outcome is the calling off of the march. He would be prepared to consider proposals along the lines thought out by S, since their adoption would in his view amount to a victory for the police – a view which only the black moderate X would dispute.

The official police statement issued just prior to the march, and published through loud-speaker vans touring the streets, announced that the police would if necessary use force to disperse the marchers. 'The streets will be cleared', the statement proclaimed, 'but in the process many marchers and some policemen are likely to be injured. Their blood and suffering will be on the hands and consciences of those who organize the march.' This statement accurately expresses the official police view. In the event the marchers were dispersed and forty of them along with three police officers were injured. Thus those who witnessed these events knew in advance the police assessment of the likely immediate consequences of their proposed action in the confrontation situation and later found these expectations confirmed. The assessment of expected immediate consequences is thus in this particular case also an assessment of the actual immediate consequences, on the assumption that the personal experience of the melée does not bring about any change in attitude towards the expected (and actual) consequences on the part of any of the participants or observers. This point is dealt with later (see p. 81). Subject to this, the attitude of our cast towards the police statement of expected consequences is summed up in Tables 4.4 and 4.5 opposite.

On march dispersal everyone accepts this as an intended consequence and all agree that it is almost certain to be realized. They hold the police directly responsible for the dispersal. One might perhaps have expected that the assessments here would have coincided with those given in Table 4.1 with columns one and two together giving those who approve of the expected and actual consequences of the march being dispersed and column three those who disapprove. However, while the Rev. W, militant Y and Black Power supporter Z do not endorse the police proposal to take action to disperse the march, they all believe in rather

Table 4.4 The police and the injury-of-marchers consequence

Police held directly responsible	Police not held directly responsible	Approve of marchers-being-injured consequence	Not approve of marchers-being-injured consequence
Rev. W	Police Chief (PC)	PC	DPC
moderate X	Deputy Chief (DPC)	B	A
militant Y	Policeman A	Rev. W	X
Black Power Z	Policeman B	Y	Q
white liberal R	Apathetic white P	Z	R
philosopher S	black defeatist Q	P	S

different ways that the negro cause will benefit from the police taking violent dispersal action. In that sense, then, they approve of the consequences. They differ in the terms of their approval or disapproval of such a consequence. Nobody argues that the police authorities intended that policemen should be injured, this projected consequence is regarded by all as an unintended but more

Table 4.5 The police and the injury-of-policemen consequence

Police held directly responsible	Police not held directly responsible	Approve of policemen-being-injured consequence	Not approve of policemen-being-injured consequence
Rev. W	Police Chief (PC)	Y	PC
militant Y	Deputy Chief (DPC)	Z	DPC
Black Power Z	Policeman A		A
white liberal R	Policeman B		B
	apathetic white P		Rev. W
	moderate X		X
	black defeatist Q		P
	philosopher S		Q
			R
			S

or less inevitable consequence of police action.[1] Where persons differ is over who is held responsible for those injuries and in the expression of approval or disapproval of such injuries being incurred. The same considerations apply with reference to the injury of marchers, although here everyone holds that the police directly intend that negroes shall be hurt, as distinct from injuries being an inevitable consequence of the form of action proposed in accordance with their belief in the accuracy of the police rumoured objective (see pp. 59, 60). The question of responsibility clearly turns on how one interprets the whole course of events and the background to them. Supporters of racial discrimination hold the negroes responsible for what happens since they 'started it' by holding the march, while its opponents hold the police responsible since they prevented the negroes from peacefully demonstrating in support of their constitutional rights.[2]

The Civil Rights moderate X, while he agrees that the police are in a broad sense responsible for all the injury consequences, holds that direct responsibility for the injury of policemen must be with those marchers who forsake non-violence and assault their assailants – a position endorsed by the Martian philosopher S. The black defeatist Q is inclined to lay direct responsibility on the Civil Rights Movement for the injuries and feels that marchers who get injured have only themselves to blame for getting involved in such a dangerous and stupid situation. Only Y and Z approve of policemen being injured, although Q would do so if it did not feel that the upshot were likely to be an increase in police harassment of negroes.

The long-term police assessment of the consequences of their action at Big Rock is clear and well-known, since their statements speak of 'the need to take action before the extremists of the Civil Rights and Black Power Movements get any stronger'. Unfortunately for them the upshot of the publicity given to the Big Rock incident (and especially the television screening of policemen clubbing passive negro demonstrators) is the suspension of the Police Chief by the State Governor, a serious lowering of police

1 It would be possible for someone like Q to argue that the Police Chief was quite happy with the prospect of having some of his own men injured, even though this was not a direct intention. He might hope that such injury would arouse public sympathy for the police and against the marcher and that it would heighten anti-civil rights feeling and solidarity within the ranks of the force.

2 For the purpose of analysis the responsibility of the magistrate in upholding the police ban of the march has been ignored.

morale and an upsurge in the influence of the Civil Rights and Black Power Movements – although the latter gains more than the former. The relationship between long-term expected consequences and actual consequences for the three bodies concerned is set out in Table 4.6, where + represents an expected or realized gain in influence and − a reduction.

Table 4.6 Assessments of long-term consequences

	Police influence Expected	Actual	CRM influence Expected	Actual	BP influence Expected	Actual
Police*	+	−	−	+	−	+ +
Civil Rights Movement (CRM)	−	−	+	+	−	+ +
Black Power (BP)	−	−	−	+ +	+	+ +

* Assessment not shared by Deputy Police Chief—see Table 4.7 below.

The publicized police assessment of long-term consequences in terms of relative influence can be looked at to see firstly whether one agrees with the assessment, i.e. whether it coincides with one's own view of the likely outcome, and secondly whether one would like to see such an outcome realized. The actual outcome can then be appraised in approval/disapproval terms. The outcome can also be used to determine whether the action taken by the police was justified in terms of the actual consequences realized. An action will be regarded as justified in terms of consequences for any of the participating bodies if the consequences secure intentions, or if, although not securing them, the consequences are beneficial or approved of.[1] These assessments are in practice likely to take a rough quantitative form of 'more' or 'less', rather than an absolute form, since consequences are rarely clear-cut. Moreover, it is very difficult to determine the extent to which the longer-term consequences which follow on a particular course of events are the direct consequence of these events. Nevertheless

1 If the consequences are not as intended and not beneficial then one has to distinguish between those cases where they result from the intervention of factors which might reasonably have been foreseen and those where they could not. In the former case the action at the time could be held to have been justified in terms of consequences then expected; but not in the latter.

people do make and have to make assessments of this kind. As far as the justification of police action in terms of longer-term consequences is concerned only the Police Chief and Police Officer B are prepared to seek to justify the action taken after the event, but in spite of, not because of, the consequences. They put the blame for the unfavourable outcome on the intervention of outside forces and argue that, if backed up by higher authorities in the city and the state, the police could have weathered the storm of protest and emerged stronger than ever in relation to their black opponents.

In analysing the attitudes towards the consequences these have

Table 4.7 Appraisal of police assessment of longer-term consequences and of actual consequences

	(i) Agree with assessment			(ii) Like to see			(iii) Pleased with actual		
	a+	b−	c−	a+	b−	c−	*a−*	b+	c++
Police Chief	√	√	√	√	√	√	×	×	×
Deputy PC	×	×	×	√	√	√	×	×	×
Police Officer A	√	√	√	√	×	√	×	√	×
Police Officer B	√	√	√	√	√	√	×	×	×
Rev. W	×	×	√	×	×	√	√	√	×
moderate X	×	×	×	×	×	√	√	√	×
militant Y	×	×	×	×	×	×	√	√	√
Black Power Z	×	√	×	×	√	×	√	×	√
apathetic white P	Don't know			√	√	√	×	×	×
black defeatist Q	√	√	√	×	×	×	√	√	√
white liberal R	×	×	×	×	×	√	√	√	×
philosopher S	×	×	×	×	×	?	?	√	?

been broken down into the three separate components: (a) the influence of the police (b) the influence of the Civil Rights Movement and (c) the influence of the Black Power Movement. Table 4.7 shows the distribution of attitudes towards the police assessments and the actual results, with √ representing a positive response and × a negative one.

The Martian philosopher finds it difficult to identify himself with simple negatives or positives to some of the positions set out in columns (ii) and (iii) of the table. While he would not himself support the use of violence, it seems to him that negro violence has been an important ingredient in drawing attention to the negroes' plight and in scaring the apathetic white population into taking some remedial action. At the same time he is not at all happy with a situation where mounting negro violence is taking place in a town where police authority is on the wane.

In the second part of this inquiry we shall be concerned with the situation as viewed from the angle of the other parties to the confrontation, the Civil Rights Movement (CRM) and Black Power Movement (BPM). The former is a loosely organized body composed of representatives of a wide range of local associations, including the moderate Southern Christian Leadership Conference, and the more militant Congress of Racial Equality. In addition there are considerable numbers of individual members. The Black Power Movement is small in numbers but tightly organized and disciplined. The authority of movements like these comes not from the state but from those who join and support them. Such movements, however, do not simply claim to speak on behalf of their members, but on behalf of the distinctive group from which their members are drawn – the negroes, where that distinctive feature is considered to be the overriding dominant and pervasive feature of their lives. Negro movements insist that they have a 'right' to the support of all negroes, i.e. a claim against negroes for their support in furtherance of negro aims and aspirations. This is expressed in terms of what the movement stands for, on the one hand, and on the other of the realizability of its objective judged by reference to the nature of the organization – its assessment of the form of the struggle, the tactics and methods to be followed and the degree of success already secured.

The Civil Rights Movement and the Black Power Movement appear as bitter competitors who nevertheless share certain common conceptions and objectives. Both seek to end the injustices and discriminations suffered by the negro in the United States and to abolish his inferior status and economic position. Negroes are seen by both movements as having an obligation to help realize this objective, an obligation to help themselves by refusing to accept their menial deprived status, and an obligation to the whole negro group of which they are members. The former obligation is not simply a prudential one, nor the latter simply a moral one – the obligation stems from the social fact of negrohood under conditions of white dominance. Those who specifically deny or reject any obligation to support the negro cause are either cowards or traitors to their blood brothers and to themselves. By denying the negro cause they are seen by both the Civil Rights and the Black Power Movements as attempting to deny themselves as negroes.

On the other hand, whereas the Civil Rights Movement bases its appraisals on the spiritual values of Christianity and the traditions of non-violent resistance to evil to secure reforms within the existing social and political system, the Black Power Movement is in the revolutionary tradition with White Power as the Black enemy. For both groups negro support is seen and claimed as necessary to ensure success, but while Black Power relies on 'ourselves alone' to overthrow white rule, the Civil Rights Movement aims to enlist support from white persons and organizations, including the Federal Government itself. The latter claims the degree of recognition it is accorded by established bodies and governmental authorities (which are predominantly white) as reasons why negroes should support it, since it augurs well for the success of the anti-discrimination cause within United States society; the former sees these same recognitions as manifestations of colour-collaboration which may secure minor improvements of the negro lot but which cannot change his servile status within society. Black Power boasts of its unacceptability to White Power and its harassment of the Police as firm evidence of the validity of its own conceptions and practices in furthering the true interests of the negro. Black leaders need to be feared, not esteemed, by white leaders.

Both bodies in their differing ways claim the self-sacrifice of their members and the incorruptibility of their leaders as grounds for negro confidence and support, and their refusal to compromise on fundamental principles and the endorsement of their position by prominent negroes as further grounds for negro approval, though each seeks to deny and undermine the validity of the other's assertions. On the basis of its own image of itself each movement makes claim to authority, in the form of claims to various forms of support which it has a right to expect from negroes generally. Although each would recognize that its own claims are unlikely to secure acceptance by all negroes, and that the extent and intensity of acceptance will vary widely, yet each would argue that, in terms of what it is and seeks to do, all negroes ought to support it. The Civil Rights Movement goes further and declares that 'all good men and true', white and black alike, ought to come to its aid.

The aims of the Civil Rights Movement may be expressed as the removal of racial discrimination in the United States through non-violent political struggle, including civil disobedience, and the Black Power Movement's as 'the realization of Black Power in the United States through revolutionary liberation of the blacks

from white domination'.[1] The Civil Rights Movement's aims are
endorsed by the movement's members (Rev. W, X and Y), the
white liberal R, and the Martian philosopher S. Police Officer A,
the black defeatist Q and the Black Power supporter Z support
the removal of racial discrimination, but not the method proposed
for its realization. A has doubts about the propriety and legality
of civil disobedience, while Z and Q do not believe civil disobedience can be effective. Unlike the former, Q has no faith in the
efficacy of any form of struggle to secure the future he would
like to see. Black Power aims are endorsed only by Z, though the
young militant Y has considerable sympathy with them.

If we now turn to the assessments of the authority of these
movements by reference to the degree of support they are thought
to possess we find that, with the exception of the Police Chief,
Police Officer B and the apathetic white P, all the other actors at
Big Rock agree that the Civil Rights Movement has the support of
the majority of negroes, in that they endorse its aims as set out
above. The Police Chief and Police Officer B insist that it is only
a small extremist minority who support the Movement, while the
apathetic P doesn't know. The Deputy Police Chief and the
Martian philosopher S both base their assessments on published
opinion poll information. The supports of the movement itself tend
to use the polls to confirm their own assessments, and are liable
to discount any evidence showing a fall-away of support. Nobody
believes that the majority of negroes support the Black Power
Movement, but everyone believes that their influence and support
is growing, though to varying degrees and for various reasons.
There is general agreement that white liberals and the Federal
Government[2] support the Civil Rights Movement but not the
Black Power Movement, although the Police Chief, and still more
Officer B, are inclined to identify white liberals with 'communists'
and 'anarchists', allies of Black Power. However, whereas most

1 The Civil Rights and Black Power Movements in the United States are
  not like orthodox political parties with authorized publicized statements
  of aims and policy. What I have given as 'aims' here are not, therefore,
  extracts from official positions, but expressions consistent with the positions
  taken up by many of those who labelled themselves supporters of these
  two movements. For discussion see Elliot M. Zachin, *Civil Disobedience
  and Democracy* (Free Press, New York, 1972); Robert L. Scott and Wayne
  Brocknide (eds), *The Rhetoric of Black Power* (Harper & Row, New York,
  1969); and Stokely Carmichael, 'Black Power', in *The Dialectics of
  Liberation* (Penguin, Harmondsworth, 1968).
2 Civil Rights Acts were passed by Congress under strong pressure from
  President Johnson in 1964 and 1965.

persons see white liberal support as a source of strength, Z sees the stress on such support as a major source of weakness in the Civil Rights Movement. Z also holds that the Federal Government pays only lip service to civil rights and anti-discrimination, while doing its best to delay implementation. Apart from the Police Chief and Officer B, who see sinister influence at work, the others regard Federal support as being more the result of Civil Rights activity and pressure, than a reflection of deep commitment to that cause. Further, Y, Q and to some extent the Rev. W have doubts about whether the Federal Government can be relied on to carry through further anti-discrimination measures. The philosopher S is troubled by the difficulty of identifying the characteristics and dimensions of the so-called 'white liberals'. He wonders whether liberal support for civil rights may not follow tautologically from defining a liberal in these terms. He resolves this dilemma for himself by distinguishing between supporting the cause of ending racial discrimination from supporting a movement to secure this end by civil disobedience means. Finally, the Civil Rights Movements' claim that their objective of ending racial discrimination is in accordance with, and required by, the constitution is accepted by all except P, the 'Don't know' apathetic white, and by the Police Chief and Officer B who deny that the constitution requires or permits interference with states' rights. They are supported by the Deputy Police Chief who argues that it is not the constitution which has changed since the adoption of the Fourteenth Amendment and the *Civil Rights Cases* (1883), but the interpretation of the constitution by the increasingly politically orientated members of the United States Supreme Court.

These assessments as to whether the Civil Rights and Black Power Movements have the support of various groups and bodies may be contrasted with assessments as to whether these movements have a 'right' to their support. Table 4.8 shows those who make different assessments of support given and support entitled to.

Q's position is simply that he does not believe that anyone has the right to claim his support for their cause. As a pessimist about men in general and negroes in particular he is unable to make the general cause his own. As a self-centred person he refuses to accept any obligation to do anything which might be burdensome or possibly dangerous to himself. The attitude of the Police Chief, his Deputy and Police Officer B is explained by their belief that all whites ought to oppose the undermining of the white-oriented and dominated society of the South. The philosopher S does not appear in Table 4.8, since he is not clear precisely how to interpret the concept of 'right to support'.

If one wants to ascertain how far 'the right to support' goes, one must look at such questions as the right to issue orders to members of the organization, and to negroes generally, the right to use sanctions against those refusing to obey orders, and the right to bring pressure and coercion to bear against those who oppose the organization and its activities. Apart from the Police Chief, Officer B and the 'Don't know' P, all other persons accept that the right to issue orders to its members is part of what is understood as involved

Table *4.8*   Difference in assessments of support given and support entitled to – Civil Rights and Black Power Movements

CRM *support of negroes* Have, but no right to it	CRM *support of white liberals* Have, but no right to it	CRM *support of Federal Govt* Have, but no right to it	BP *support of negroes* Not have, but a right to it
Z Q	Police Chief Deputy Officer B P* Q	Police Chief Deputy P Q	Y Z

* 'Don't know' on having support.

in being a member of an organization. This is seen as applying to both the Civil Rights and Black Power Movements. The only reservation comes from the moderate black X who insists that each member has the right and responsibility to determine for himself whether any order he is given is morally unacceptable. He accepts, however, a *prima facie* obligation to obey orders.

The ultimate sanction which anyone is prepared to consider using against those who disobey Civil Rights Movement orders is expulsion, but Z is prepared to see physical sanctions (such as a beating-up) used against a Black Power member who fails to carry out an important assignment. X will not accept a right of the Civil Rights Movement to issue orders to negroes who are not members of the movement and who may not even support it. Only the Rev. W, the militant Y and the liberal R therefore assert such a right for the Civil Rights Movement and only Z for the Black

Power Movement. No question of sanctions against non-members who do not obey orders arises for the former, as the only morally acceptable sanction, expulsion, is not applicable to non-members. While for Z the situation is not likely to occur often he does not rule out the use of force or the threat of force against outsiders who refuse to carry out specific and important orders e.g. to provide weapons or money for a jail-break. Z is prepared to bring pressure to bear against those who will not support his cause, and in the last resort would support coercion against those who strongly oppose the Black Power Movement. Within the Civil Rights Movement no one would countenance physical violence against opponents, though the Rev. W and still more the militant Y, would support the use of the pressure of organized opinion against opponents (including ostracism and boycott in Y's case), but not against non-supporters.

In sharp contrast, the majority of those involved at Big Rock would accept the right of negro organizations to use sanctions, including force, against police informers within their ranks. Only the Police Chief, Officer B and the non-violent X are opposed, though X would support public exposure and personal ostracism. Even the two police officers, while denying a 'right' to act, agree that negroes who 'rat' on their own people by informing to the police 'deserve' all they get. Different persons have different ideas about the amount and purpose of the coercion to be applied in such cases. The Deputy Police Chief, Rev. W and philosopher S would only countenance the threat or use of force to make informers divulge what they have passed on, while A, Y, Z, P, Q and R see physical force as merited punishment. Nobody likes informers. When one turns to the threat or use of force for other purposes we find that Rev. W, Y, Z, Q, R and S accept a 'right' to use coercion as a protection against police violence, reducing to Y, Z, Q, R for retaliation to police violence. Y and Z stand alone in claiming a 'right' to provoke police violence. Both, however, would argue that such actions would be designed simply to bring out into the open the violence existing within the White Power system and would put the blame for the violence provoked firmly on the police themselves. Z would go further and claim for Black Power a 'right' to cause any disruption or violent incident deemed necessary to further the cause.

Finally, before turning to the position of the negro organizations in the confrontation at Big Rock, we shall look at the 'credit-worthiness' of the Civil Rights and Black Power Movements, as expressed through opinions on the devotion and dedication of the members of the organization to the realization of their stated aims and principles, and the incorruptibility of their leaders (imperviousness to bribery, flattery or pressure). On the first point there is full positive agreement, though the Police Chief and Officer B are inclined to see more sinister aims and objectives lying behind the stated purposes. On the second point these two officers cannot accept that the leaders are incorruptible, it is simply that ways have not yet been found to corrupt them. This view on corruptibility is endorsed by the black defeatist Q with regard to the Civil Rights Movement but not to the Black Power Movement. Q's view, also held by the Deputy Police Chief and the Black Power supporter Z, is that the leaders of the former organization might well be 'bought off' or 'persuaded' to compromise on their basic aims and principles, whereas the leaders of the more militant and highly organized Black Power Movement are fanatics who could not be. The philosopher S takes the view that it is largely the nature of the Black Power Movement that makes its leaders impervious to corruption from without. He does not rule out internal corruption, the seeking of personal power at the expense of the good of the movement, though not with any anti-movement purpose in view. He holds the view that the leaders of the Civil Rights Movement are not corrupt, but because of the nature of their stand, they are much more likely to be caught up in the ordinary political processes of compromise and bargaining, and are therefore very vulnerable to accusations of corruption from disappointed members who will not be satisfied with half a loaf. Thus in addition to A, Rev. W, X, Y, R and S, who hold the Civil Rights and Black Power Movements' leaders to be 'not corruptible', the Deputy Police Chief, Z and Q take this view in respect of Black Power only. P remains a 'Don't know'.

The confrontation situation at Big Rock will be looked at in the same terms for the negro organizations as for the police viz. aims and objectives, methods proposed for realizing the objectives, immediate and longer-term consequences. The stated and publicized objective *s.o.* of the Civil Rights Movement in organizing the march in spite of police banning, is to demonstrate negro support for the civil rights cause and as a protest against the ban itself. The widely rumoured and accurate belief is that their objective *r.o.* is to confront the police with the alternatives of either giving way and permitting the march, or having to disperse it with force. As far as the Black Power Movement is concerned its stated objective *s.o.* is that negroes on the march should defend themselves from attacks by the police, the rumoured and actual objective *r.o.* is to provoke fights between negroes and police. In each case the rumoured objective goes beyond the stated objective but is not inconsistent with it.

All those involved in the incident hold that *r.o.* incorporates *s.o.* and that the rumoured objective is in fact the actual objective in both cases. They do not necessarily accept that the realization of *r.o.* would mean realization of *s.o.*: simply that those who endorse *r.o.* also endorse *s.o.* The positions taken up are shown in Table 4.9.

Table 4.9   Civil Rights Movement and Black Power Movement objectives

endorse *s.o.* endorse *r.o.* of	endorse *s.o.* reject *r.o.* of	reject *s.o.* reject *r.o.* of
(i) Civil Rights Movement		
Rev. W	Police Officer A	Police Chief
militant Y	moderate X	Deputy
Black Power Z	white liberal R	Police Officer B
	philosopher S	apathetic white P
		black defeatist Q
(ii) Black Power Movement		
Y	Rev. W	Police Chief
Z	R	Deputy
		Officers A and B
		X, P, Q

Apart from Q, who as a defeatist does not support any action directed against established authority, those who reject the rumoured objective of the Civil Rights Movement do so because they feel it conflicts with the stated commitment of the movement to non-violence. Though the Martian philosopher S does not necessarily commit himself to the non-violence principle, he feels that the movement has, and that he cannot endorse such a fundamental inconsistency.

After the Police Chief has ordered the marchers to disperse, the Civil Rights leader, Rev. W, and the march marshals tell all marchers to sit down quietly and wait: 'Don't do anything, just sit and show the people of Big Rock and the whole United

States that we shall not be moved.' Z and other Black Power supporters issue leaflets declaring 'Don't sit on your arse while the pigs beat in your head. Stand up and fight for your rights. Arm yourselves with sticks and stones. Tell the white pigs to go home if they don't want to get hurt.' Everyone accepts that Black Power tactics, in association with those pursued by the police, are in the circumstances likely to lead to the achievement of the rumoured objective – provoking fights between negroes and police. Only Y and Z believe that these tactics hold out the remote possibility that the majority of those on the march will stand up to the police and defend themselves when attacked. It may be argued that for the Black Power Movement the achievement of *s.o.* is not

Table 4.10 Assessment of effectiveness of CRM tactics for realizing stated and rumoured objectives

Effective for *s.o.*	Not effective for *s.o.*	Effective for *r.o.*	Not effective for *r.o.*
Deputy Police Chief	Police Chief	Police Chief	Deputy Police Chief
Officer A	Officer B	Officer B	Officer A
Rev. W	Q	Rev. W	X
X		Q	Y
Y		R	Z
Z		S	
R			
S			

necessary for the realization of *r.o.*, although it is not an alternative to it. Thus one might say that nobody holds that the proposed tactics are likely to secure Black Power's *s.o.* and that everyone believes they will produce (or help produce) the *r.o.*

The position is more complicated with the Civil Rights Movement, as can be seen from Table 4.10 (P is excluded as a 'Don't know').

The Police Chief, Officer B and the black defeatist Q do not expect that the outcome of the march confrontation will be a demonstration of the strength of support for the civil rights' cause. On the other hand all three of them believe that the tactics proposed will help to bring about the confrontation situation, where the only alternatives are police capitulation or forceful dispersal. This view is shared by the Rev. W, the liberal R and philosopher S, given the nature of the stand already taken up by the Police Chief. Those who take an opposing view do so on the qualified grounds that such tactics need not necessarily lead to the confrontation situation. The initiative under 'sit and see' tactics rests with the police who could decide to avoid the sharp alternatives envisaged by the Rev. W and his colleagues. It is the avoidance of the confrontation which the Deputy Police Chief, Officer A and black moderate X are seeking and which Y and Z want to make certain.

The assessments of the legitimacy of the action proposed by the Civil Rights and Black Power Movements to secure their stated and

Table 4.11   Assessment of validity of proposed action by the Civil Rights Movement and the Black Power Movement to secure their objectives

| | Civil Rights Movement | | | Black Power Movement | |
| | *s.o.* | | *r.o.* | *s.o.* and *r.o.* | |
Action justified	Not justified	Justified	Not justified	Justified	Not justified
A	PC	W	PC	X	PC
W	DPC	Y	DPC	Z	DPC
X	B	Z	A	Q	A
Y	P	Q	B		B
Z			X		W
Q			P		X
R			R		P
S			S		R
					S

rumoured objectives is set out in Table 4.11, where 'justification' refers to the use of the means proposed to secure stated and rumoured objectives (see p. 61).

If this table is compared with Table 4.9 it will be noted that the black defeatist Q, who did not endorse the stated or rumoured objectives of either the Civil Rights or Black Power Movements, holds that such actions directed against the established authorities, although unwise, are certainly justified. The other difference is that Rev. W, the white liberal R and Martian philosopher S, who endorsed the stated objective of the Black Power Movement, do not believe that the action proposed by that movement is justified, since it goes beyond simple unarmed defence against police attack to armed resistance with sticks and stones. As a result the assessments of action to secure stated and rumoured objectives are the same for the Black Power Movement.

The Civil Rights Movement and the Black Power Movement make the same appraisal as the Police of the immediate consequences likely to result from the confrontation situation – the dispersal of the march, the injury of a considerable number of negro marchers and of some policemen. Their public statements, while less bold than that of the Police Chief, make this plain to all. 'If the Police of Big Rock insist on using the evil of naked force against us', proclaims the Civil Rights manifesto 'they will be able to win the battle of the streets since we shall not resist. Many of our people may suffer injury at police hands and some hotheads in spite of our warnings may retaliate and injure policemen. But we shall win the war for our rights by gaining the moral and political support of the majority of citizens of the United States.' The Black Power Movement's statement is somewhat shorter. 'Black brothers they may break the heads of those who stupidly refuse to retaliate, and force us off the streets, but those who follow us will have the satisfaction of having felled some of the white pigs and of having raised the banner of the Black Power struggle in Big Rock.' This coincidence of the assessments of expected consequences of both negro movements with that of the police, as we have seen above (p. 62) finds confirmation in the actual situation realized on the ground. The issues not explored above relate to the extent to which the Civil Rights Movement or the Black Power Movement are held responsible for these consequences, or held to have intended to bring them about.

Neither the Civil Rights Movement nor the Black Power Movement are held directly and immediately responsible for the march being dispersed – everyone having accepted that the police are responsible for this. However, the Police Chief, his Deputy, Officer B, the apathetic white P and the black defeatist Q, hold that the Civil Rights Movement has an overriding responsibility for the march being dispersed, in that they organized it in the first place, in spite of its being banned. The philosopher S, though at first impressed by the force of this argument, feels that it might equally be argued that it was the police ban of the march which was responsible for the marchers being dispersed. Once one moves beyond assessments of direct responsibility there is no end to the list of possible candidates for indirect or prior responsibility.

Further complications arise when one turns to the question of whether the Civil Rights Movement 'intended' the marchers to be forcibly dispersed. Everyone accepted that the real objective of the movement had been to face the police with the alternatives of either (a) giving way and allowing the march to continue, or (b) forcibly dispersing it. In one sense, therefore, all accept that the movement intended this as one of two desired alternatives. However, there is a difference to be found in terms of whether (b) was felt to be the preferred alternative, or the only seriously considered alternative; (a) having been ruled out as completely unrealizable in the circumstances prevailing. The distinction becomes one between those who believe that the Civil Rights Movement 'really wanted' to have the march dispersed and those who feel they 'really wanted' the police to give way. The former view is that held by the Deputy Police Chief, Rev. W, the militant Y, Black Power supporter Z, the black defeatist Q and the Martian philosopher S, the latter view by the Police Chief, Officers A and B, the black moderate X, and the apathetic white P and white liberal R. As far as the Black Power Movement is concerned nobody holds that it intended the march to be dispersed – rather it intended the marchers to fight back. Ideally they would overwhelm the police and march in triumph through the streets, though this was not thought to be an achievable objective.

Of these who do not hold the police directly responsible for the injury of marchers (Table 4.4), the Police Chief, Officer B, apathetic white P and black defeatist Q hold the two negro movements equally responsible, while the Deputy Police Chief and Officer A lay direct responsibility on the Black Power Movement alone. The same persons who hold that the Civil Rights Movement 'intended' in some sense that the march should be dispersed, also hold that it 'intended' that negro marchers should be injured. The Deputy Police Chief, Black Power supporter Z and the black defeatist Q take the strong view that the movement's leaders wanted negro heads 'blooded' in order to arouse public protest and further their campaign and influence. The Rev. W, the militant Y and the philosopher S hold the weaker view that negro injuries were not directly intended, but accepted as a likely outcome which could be turned to the movement's advantage. Similarly the Deputy Police Chief, Officer A, Rev. W, moderate X, the Black defeatist Q, and liberal white R, believe that the Black Power Movement directly intended that negroes should get hurt through the tactics it pursued, while militant Y and Black Power member Z simply accept this as a likely outcome of Black Power tactics.

The philosopher wavers between the two positions, seeing negro injuries as a necessary rather than directly intended outcome.

Opinions on the responsibility for, and intentions of, the two negro movements for the injury to policemen are easier to disentangle and are set out in Table 4.12. It is worth noting that, while the Rev. W and white liberal R hold the police responsible for what happens, including the injuries to policemen (see Table 4.5), they accept, after the experience of the particular events, that the Black Power Movement must bear a degree of respon-

Table 4.12 Injury of policemen: responsibility and intentions of the Civil Rights and Black Power Movements

	Civil Rights Movement		Black Power Movement	
	Responsible for injuries	Intended the injuries	Responsible for injuries	Intended the injuries
Police Chief	PC	PC	PC	PC
Deputy Police Chief	B		DPC	DPC
Officer B	P		A	A
apathetic white P			B	B
defeatist black Q			Rev. W	Rev. W
			X	X
			P	Y
			Q	Z
			R	P
			S	Q
				R
				S

sibility for these occurrences. Y and Z take up the extreme position of accepting that the Black Power Movement intended to injure policemen, but lay responsibility on the police for the injuries, since they could have avoided them, either by allowing the march or by individual police officers keeping out of the marchers' way.

We may complete the picture by looking at the appraisals of the assessments made by the Civil Rights and Black Power Movements of the longer-term consequences of the Big Rock incident, completing the pictures presented in Table 4.7 of the assessments of the police. It will be remembered that the assessments of all those bodies were made under the headings (a) influence of the police, (b) influence of the Civil Rights Movement and (c) the influence of the Black Power Movement. The Civil Rights Movement assessment was a— b+ c— and the Black Power assessment a— b— c+. The actual outcome was a— b+ c++ (see Table 4.6). Table 4.13 shows how the persons at Big Rock judged these assessments, before the event, as likely outcomes and as outcomes they would like to see realized.

We may now consider the particular incidents enacted by our cast. When the Police Chief gives the order to disperse, the Rev. W orders the marchers to sit down. Z tries to persuade those around

Table 4.13 Appraisal of the Civil Rights and Black Power Movements' assessments of longer-term consequences of Big Rock incident

| | Civil-Rights-Movement assessment | | | | | | Black-Power-Movement assessment | | | | | |
| | Agree with | | | Like to see | | | Agree with | | | Like to see | | |
	a—	b+	c—	a—	b+	c—	a—	b—	c+	a—	b—	c+
Police Chief	×	×	√	×	×	√	×	√	×	×	√	×
Deputy	√	√	×	×	×	√	√	×	√	×	√	×
Officer A	×	×	√	×	√	√	×	√	×	×	×	×
Officer B	×	×	√	×	×	√	×	√	×	×	√	×
Rev. W	√	√	√	√	√	√	√	×	×	√	×	×
moderate X	√	√	×	√	√	√	√	×	√	√	×	×
militant Y	√	√	√	√	√	×	√	√	√	√	√	√
Black Power Z	√	×	×	√	×	×	√	√	√	√	√	√
apathetic white P	Don't know			×	×	√	Don't know			×	√	×
black defeatist Q	×	×	√	√	√	×	×	√	×	×	×	√
white liberal R	√	√	×	√	√	√	√	×	√	√	×	×
philosopher S*	√	√	×	?	√	?	√	×	√	?	×	?

* See note on philosopher's position p. 61 above.

him to march forward against the police, arming themselves with sticks and stones. Only Y is prepared to join him, so they content themselves with abusing the police as 'fascist pigs'. Ten minutes pass and the Police Chief gives the order to charge. Police Officer B rushes forward and lashes out at the seated moderate X. On witnessing this the enraged young militant Y fells Police Officer B and then hits Police Officer A who has been trying to persuade seated marchers to disperse. Y and Z run away into the crowd of observers. Dazed and maddened, Officer B drags the unfortunate X to his feet and very forcibly arrests him without any resistance on X's part. These events are seen by all cast members. Only the Police Chief approves of Police Officer B hitting the sitting X, although the apathetic white P thinks it serves X right for being there. B's action in arresting X is approved of not only by the Police Chief and P but by the Deputy Police Chief and Officer A, although both feel that he ought not to, and need not have, roughly handled him in doing so. Only Z approves of Y hitting Police Officer A and this action leads the white liberal R to modify his view that the police must be held directly responsible for injuries to their members (see Table 4.5). Y's action in knocking down Officer B is approved, with some reservations, by the black defeatist bystander, Q, as well as by Z. The Civil Rights leader, Rev. W, wavers on the issue but finally comes down against. X's two actions in not defending himself against attack and not resisting arrest surprisingly produce very different responses. Only Police Officer A approves of the former, while the latter is disapproved of by only Y and Z. The philosopher admires X's equanimity in face of attack but does not approve, since it appears to provoke men like Officer B to acts of aggression, rather than act as a deterrent. For most persons, including Officer B, a failure to defend oneself against attack appears as unnatural and unmanly.

Finally an attempt should be made to see if it is possible to distinguish between 'approved of' and 'justified' action and between the latter and 'understandable' action. Your action will be assessed as 'approved' if I am pleased that it has occurred, and as 'justified' if I might well have done the same myself, if I were *myself* in your position.[1] This may be contrasted with 'understandable' action as action which I would not myself have done in your position, but action which I can conceive of someone in your position doing, where being in your position is not something I find inconceivable or completely unacceptable. All three classes of action comprise actions which I am prepared to defend in their own terms. 'Justified' and 'Understandable' are positions which are mutually exclusive. Table 4.14 summarizes these different appraisals.

The Martian philosopher S finds himself in the somewhat unenviable position of finding all these human actions 'understandable'

[1] If alternatively I attempt an assessment in terms of being *him* in his position, this means I see the choices as he sees them. Strictly applied this will mean that the action will always appear as justified, except in so far as he made an error of judgment which he might have avoided. More immediately and practically, assessments of this kind can rarely if ever be made because we don't know sufficient about the other participants to be able to put ourselves into their shoes with their personalities, values and capacities. Moreover, at the extreme we cannot conceive of ourselves in these terms (as a Nazi torturer for example) and we refuse to do so because it eliminates the possibility of any moral judgment.

in terms of what he knows about the participants and their positions in the confrontation situation, but he does not 'approve' of any of the actions and finds only the non-resisting of arrest 'justified'. Although Q 'approves' of Y hitting B he does not think it 'justified', in that as a defeatist he cannot conceive of himself committing such an action. Z, the Black Power member, is

Table 4.14 Assessment of particular actions

	'Approved'	'Justified'	'Understandable'
Police Officer B hits X	Police Chief	Police Chief P	Deputy Police Chief S
Y hits Police Officer A	Z	Z	Rev. W Q R S
Y hits Police Officer B	Z Q	Z R Rev. W	Deputy Police Chief A X S Q
B arrests X	Police Chief Deputy A P	Police Chief Deputy A P	X S
X not defend himself	A	A R	Deputy Police Chief Rev. W, Y S
X not resist arrest	All save Y and Z	Rev. W, A R S Deputy Police Chief	Y Q S Police Chief, B Z

associated with the Police Chief and Officer B, the black defeatist Q and the apathetic white P in not 'understanding' why X does not defend himself when attacked by B – they cannot conceive of themselves acting in that way. But they can all 'understand' why X does not resist arrest, although the Police Chief, Officer B and Z cannot imagine themselves getting into this particular situation.

Conclusion

Although the political drama at Big Rock was designed to permit an analysis of the complex ingredients of confrontation situations, it has to be recognized that the process of 'staging' necessarily introduces artificiality. In any actual confrontation it is doubtful whether opposing leaders, front rank contestants and observers would all have received the same information and observed the same occurrences when making their assessments of events. It is unlikely that they would all have access to and all believe the same accounts regarding the rumoured objectives of the police and the two negro organizations; or that they would all have the same experience, and give the same factual account of what happened in the confrontation situation. However, this is only to recognize the difficulties which persons labour under in making political assessments and does not invalidate the analysis itself. Further I would argue that in political confrontations which arise out of conscious political activity (in contrast to 'happenings'), it is usually not difficult to know what the contestants are seeking to achieve. Their objectives are not and cannot be kept secret, they arise out of the nature of what the bodies concerned are and what they do in the particular situation.

A more serious objection which might be raised is that persons involved in such a situation would not attempt to make, or be able to make, a detailed conceptual analysis in terms of the authority of the bodies involved, their objectives, methods and consequences. If the participants are unwilling, unable, or not concerned to assess the events they are involved in, then this paper has no merit except to suggest how politically rational men *might* behave if they were ever to enter and dominate the political arena. If people do not think and appraise in anything like the fashion suggested, then confrontation situations are best analysed in quite different terms. It must be noted, however, that my analysis does not require that all men, or even all direct participants, should reflect and judge precisely in the sort of terms outlined; but simply that many of them, and especially the most active and influential, approach such situations in this kind of way. The evidence here is necessarily far from conclusive. Partly it is to be found in the increasing volume of survey material about people's attitudes to conflict situations and issues,[1] partly on personal experience and appreciation of the way men behave in politics. Men, in my view, do seek to understand the events they are involved in or which concern them, and the questions they ask are basically the same questions that are asked by more sophisticated analysts – who is involved? what are they like? what do they want? how will they act? what will be the outcome? Such questions are asked in the main not out of curiosity but to secure information, which on the basis of each person's own

1 See for example the detailed material gathered together by Gary T. Marx in the 124 tables of *Protest and Prejudice: A Study of Belief in the Black Community* (Harper & Row, New York, 1967), based on interviews conducted with over 1,100 negroes in the most important urban negro centres in the USA by the National Opinion Research Centre at the University of Chicago.

values and beliefs, position and interest, will enable him to make a judgment on the developing situation, both overall and in its several parts. In support of this thesis I would argue then that political confrontation situations in western countries commonly assume the general form that I have outlined, and that in such situations the kind of questions I have raised are relevant precisely because the leading figures, and many of their supporters and of the more interested observers, ask questions designed to elicit information and make assessments of the kind I have discussed.

The particular model used here is designed to show how political conflict situations may be analysed in terms of the ways different persons and groups of persons with differing values, attitudes, positions and interests perceive such situations and act out of their perceptions. It will be readily apparent that a white policeman in the Deep South who believes in the need to maintain white supremacy over the blacks (Policeman B) will necessarily approach and see the issues in Big Rock quite differently from the majority of negroes or white liberals. Holding the views that he does, and being the man he is, Policeman B is not open to persuasion by any of the kinds of argument that might be deployed by white liberals or black Civil Rights supporters. He would in all probability refuse to listen to their arguments, or if he heard them simply reject them out of hand. Few people are readily shifted from their fundamental standpoints. It does not follow from this, however, that fundamental positions are necessarily rigid and fixed, still less that all those with the same fundamental attitudes and values take up the same stand on questions of application. The Police Chief and his Deputy are both white segregationists but their approach to the negro problem is very different. It would be possible for the Deputy to criticize the Chief's assessments either in terms of whether they further their shared values, or in terms of the efficacy or validity of the methods proposed to secure police objectives and of the likely outcome of events.[1]

1 Changes in attitude may be brought about by the experience of the confrontation itself. Thus it would be plausible to suggest that the suspension of the Police Chief from office might lead to the resignation of Officer B to join the group of apathetic whites; while if the Chief had not been suspended Officer A's experiences of police brutality would have led him to resign. The success of negro militancy could lead Y into the Black Power camp, the Rev. W to move further along the direct confrontation path and the moderate X to gradually drop out of activity. The next stage in the negro political struggle in Big Rock would thus be played out not only in external conditions which would have changed, but by actors whose own values and conceptions had been altered by the confrontation they took part in.

Those directly involved in a confrontation incident are moved (indeed may feel under a sense of obligation), to determine who bears responsibility for actions and consequences. Difficult questions of degrees of responsibility, of indirect or underlying responsibility, are raised both for those determined to lay blame at a particular door and for those moved to disentangle the skeins of responsibility in a complex situation. Personal concern is even more apparent when one notes the extent to which those involved in, or actually observing, an incident (even indirectly via the news media) express 'approval' or 'disapproval', judge it 'justified 'or 'unjustified', 'understandable' or 'incomprehensible'. When I make such a judgment it means that I put myself in the position of those I hold responsible for the action concerned and that I am prepared to defend in the relevant terms the action they took. Such political judgments, though made by a particular individual, are not felt to be without general relevance. When the white Liberal R asserts that the black militant Y was justified in hitting Police Officer B, after the latter had hit the seated non-violent negro demonstrator X, he is not simply saying that he himself might well have acted likewise in Y's position; he is also arguing, or is willing to argue, for this interpretation against other possible or actual interpretations, as the most reasonable and appropriate one for men to make. He will recognize, however, that while some persons, like the negro defeatist Q and the Martian philosopher S, may be open to persuasion, others such as the Police Chief would not be. The latter's whole attitude towards the participants in the confrontation rules out for him any possibility of the demonstrators being justified in anything they do either individually or collectively to further their objectives.

The characters used in the Big Rock exercise were introduced as representatives of the range of views to be found in the United States on the Civil Rights issue, and as representatives of the bodies involved in the confrontation. A different confrontation situation would throw up representatives of a different range of views and of involved bodies, but a vital role would always remain for the Martian philosopher. He serves to show how a self-interested, rational individual without loyalties or ties might judge the issues involved; but where he is fully aware of his liability to transformation at any time into the form and the position of a member of any one of the parties involved in the dispute. In the dispute over private hospital beds in National Health Service (NHS) hospitals he could be made liable to find himself becoming a hospital consultant, a private patient, a NHS patient or even the Minister of Health and Social Security. I do not want to suggest that the Martian's judgment is in some strict sense the 'correct' one, or that it provides the 'answer' to the problem concerned. What I am suggesting is that the Martian position can be established to provide an objective but concerned assessment of a confrontation situation which may be regarded roughly as 'fair'.[1] His position can provide a base with which the position of directly interested parties can be compared, and may indicate whether there is any possibility of securing a resolution of the conflict which is not simply acceptable to some of the parties but which has claims to acceptance on grounds of fairness. It may be that the Martian would be found to have no role in some confrontation situations; not simply because there was no common ground between the Martian philosopher and any of the other major parties; but more fundamentally because it was impossible to conceive what the conditions would be to make him 'work', or what his answers would be to the key questions put. Even here, however, the exercise would not have been wasted, since it would have established that one was dealing with a dispute where no objectively 'fair' assessment appeared possible.

The actors in a confrontation react to a specific situation on the prior basis of their assessment of the standing of the particular parties to the dispute. It is, therefore, first necessary to establish these prior assessments. Since political confrontations always involve, directly or indirectly, the state, it will be necessary in every case to start off by establishing the attitude of the actors to the claimed authority of the specific state body involved – usually the police and/or the courts. To secure this one needs to ascertain the attitude of each actor in turn (including the police chiefs and police officers involved) to questions designed to elicit their conception of the nature and extent of police authority. I have suggested that this can best be ascertained by reference first to their views on the relevant functions of the police (maintaining law and order, enforcing the law, carrying out court decisions), in terms of whether such functions are seen as valid and necessary and whether they are carried out effectively, conscientiously and fairly. The second

1 'Fair' in this context is established by reference to the choice made of the kinds of change in position, role, qualities etc. to which the Martian philosopher S is made subject. Practical problems and philosophical problems of identity can for this purpose be ignored – one simply assumes that S 'knows' he is liable to change in the ways laid down and 'knows' that he will be the same person after the change.

batch of questions concerns attitudes to the right of the police chiefs to give different sorts of orders to their officers and to members of the public. Finally, one needs to see whether the police are regarded as entitled to use coercion in various kinds of situation. The specific forms of orders and means of coercion will have to be related to the particular confrontation situation, but it will be necessary to make use of a wide range of questions to enable one to distinguish the position of different respondents.[1] I would expect, however, that the authority of the police or other official bodies would be analysed in essentially the same framework as I have outlined above and used in Big Rock.

When one turns to actor assessment of the other parties to confrontation concerned the situation is rather different; in that it will probably be necessary to tailor the framework from incident to incident to fit the actual parties involved (in my case the Civil Rights Movement and the Black Power Movement). However, it should be possible to use essentially the same method of approach to determine the extent of the authority of each of the parties in the eyes of the actors. This I have suggested can be secured in the following manner. First, one elicits the response of each actor in turn to the claims made by those parties to their *right* to the support of the public or, more often, some specific group within it.[2] Second, one needs to find out to what extent the actors endorse or reject the broad aims and purposes of each party, and whether they see such aims and purposes as compatible with the maintenance of the existing constitution. This needs to be supplemented with assessments of the extent to which the actor believes that each party has support from the groups whose support it is claiming the *right* to have, whether that support is thought to be growing or declining, and what support it is thought to have from other interested parties or bodies (including the state agencies or government leaders). In each case one will want to know both whether the actor feels that support *is* forthcoming and whether the party has a *right* to that support. Fourth, each actor is required to determine whether, in his view, the party concerned has the right to issue

1 For 'Bad Day at Big Rock' I elicited responses to the right of the police to use coercion in carrying out their duties, against a person refusing to obey police orders, against a person disturbing the peace, a person resisting arrest and against a person he is ordered to use force against by a superior officer. Responses were required by all actors, including police chiefs and police officers.
2 I found it necessary to leave each actor to determine 'for himself' (i.e. according to how and what I had made him) what he understood by a 'right' in this context.

orders to members of its own organization and to members of groups which it claims the right to receive support from; whether it has the right to use sanctions against those refusing to obey orders, and the right to bring pressure and coercion to bear against those who oppose it (including the police). Last, actors will be asked to judge the devotion and dedication of the members of the party concerned and the incorruptibility of its leaders. From these elements one builds up a picture of the nature of the authority claimed by the non-state organizations involved and the attitude of the actors towards those claims.

One can then proceed to an analysis of the confrontation situation itself, starting with an actor by actor appraisal of the immediate aims and objectives of each party (e.g. police, CRM and BPM) to the confrontation (e.g. the banned march) in terms of endorsement or rejection.[1] In this paper I have stressed that in many cases it will be necessary to draw a distinction between 'stated' objective and 'rumoured' objective. I assumed, in my example that 'stated' + 'rumoured' = real objective, but this is unlikely normally to be the case. One might need to give a number of 'possible' or 'rumoured' objectives and ask actors to pick which they thought was the 'real' objective.

Having established each actor's views on the 'stated' and 'believed real' objectives, we can find out whether they believe that the methods proposed (or evidently to be used) are likely to be effective in each case, and whether their use for such objectives is 'justified' (what I myself might well have done if I were still *myself* but was in their position). One will proceed to try and establish what each of the parties expects to follow from the use of the methods it proposes, distinguishing between consequences it intends and those it does not intend, but which seem likely or even necessary consequences. The actors are then asked whether they accept the party's assessments of intended and unintended consequence and whether in each case they would hold the party responsible if these consequences were realized. Lastly they would be asked to say whether they would approve or not of such consequences coming to pass. In so far as the actual immediate consequences differed from those expected, one would have to repeat this stage of the exercise.

Finally it is necessary to establish actor assessment of the long-term consequences, both as judged by the parties before the event (and therefore influencing the way they conduct themselves

1 'Endorse' here means 'like to see realized'.

in preparing for the confrontation) and after it.[1] Actors are asked whether they agree with these prior judgments and whether they would like to see them realized, and after the event whether they are pleased at the actual outcome. I have expressed the long-term consequences in simple terms of an increase or decrease in the influence of each party *vis-à-vis* the other parties, and though this is likely to be adequate in a number of cases, in others the consideration of more specific consequences might be required.

I am well aware that the model I have put forward for handling the complex issues involved in political confrontation situations will almost certainly need to be revised in the light of discussion and experience in applying it. I believe, however, that the basic approach is sound and that this is demonstrated by the way it fits Bad Day at Big Rock. The next task is to proceed to an analysis of actual political confrontations, to see how far it works in the untidy world of political realities and whether it opens up any possibilities for predicting outcomes or resolving conflicts.

1 'Longer-term' consequences might be a more appropriate description, since I am not alluding to ultimate goals, but to what a party expects will be the results of this confrontation situation when these work themselves out.

5 Rights of Persons and the Liberal Tradition

RUTH ANNA PUTNAM

Among English-speaking people, and to a somewhat lesser extent among Europeans in general, it has been customary for centuries to express both social and political aspirations and political protest by way of claiming that persons, as persons, have certain rights. In the years since World War II, philosophers have again and again discussed the concept of a right: the literature is comprehensive and on the whole enlightening. In this paper, we shall not review this literature, nor deal with the questions, interesting though they are, to which it addresses itself.

The term 'rights' is highly ambiguous. There are, for example, constitutional rights, and these are of two kinds. There are the rights specifically granted to citizens, or to citizens satisfying certain further requirements – the right to equal protection under the law, the right to vote. There are, secondly, the limits placed on possible legislation, or possible subjects of legislation – 'Congress shall make no laws. . . .' We might call the latter 'liberties,' but for our purposes the distinction does not matter. This paper is not concerned with constitutional rights, although when political aspirations are expressed as rights-claims, it is generally intended that these rights be incorporated into a legal system. Nor are we concerned with rights specifically granted by law – the right to strike, the right to collect unemployment insurance payments.

Other rights accrue to an individual in virtue of his status, profession or special skills. Legislators, duly elected, have the right to sit in Congress, to speak, to introduce bills and to vote on proposed legislation. They also have rights not so clearly tied to the performance of their duties, such as the right to park their automobiles in certain designated areas. Physicians, lawyers and licensed electricians have special rights because they are physicians, lawyers or licensed electricians. These too are rights with which we are not concerned. Finally, persons have rights because they stand in certain special relationships to other persons. Some of these rights – those arising from a valid contract or a valid will – are legally enforceable, while others – those arising from promises – are not.

90

Possibly persons have rights against specific other persons because they stand in certain biological, emotional, or even accidental relationships. None of these rights are the rights which we shall examine in this paper, although it may well be that a careful analysis of the concept of having a right as it occurs in these various contexts would throw light on the notion with which we are exclusively concerned.

The rights with which we are concerned have been called natural rights, human rights, rights of men, rights of individuals; we shall generally speak of rights of persons.[1] Historically these rights have not always been carefully distinguished from, e.g. the rights of Englishmen. Nor have all human beings in the biological sense been regarded as persons. When one appeals to such rights in contemporary discussions, the intent is either to include additional human beings in the class of persons (blacks, women, children) or to widen the range of goods to which all persons are said to have a right (medical care, a minimum income).

These rights of persons used to be said to be God-given, but even in the writings of Hobbes and Locke we find utilitarian, or at any rate teleological, arguments for specific rights. Today the arguments are either teleological, i.e. broadly utilitarian, or else the claim is that these rights, whatever they may be, are self-evident. Historically, they included rights to life, liberty, property, the pursuit of happiness. There always was, and still is, a curious relationship between rights-claims and claims to equality. One is almost tempted to say that all men are equal in the sense that they have equal rights, and at the same time that they have equal rights (or even the particular rights they have) because they are equal. We mention this relationship here only because one large class of rights-claims today are phrased as claims to equality, e.g., equal rights for women, equal opportunity, and so on. We shall return to the question of equality.

One says that persons *qua* persons have certain rights when one intends to advocate that these rights be legally recognized and enforced, or when one intends to protest the systematic violation of these rights. In short, rights-claims are put forward when one judges that a situation is *bad* and that it could be *improved* by certain changes in the legal system. Thus rights-claims are value-judg-

---

1 Although rights of persons do not belong to a person because of any particular relationship in which he stands to specific other persons, we shall see later that the theory of which the doctrine of rights of persons is a part assumes that persons stand to one another in a certain relationship, namely that they are equal competitors for a limited supply of goods.

ments. In order to have a basis from which to examine rights-claims and the doctrine that persons have rights, it is necessary to adopt some view concerning the status of value-judgments in general.[1]

I shall follow a suggestion due to John Dewey[2] and consider value-judgments in general and rights-claims in particular as analogous to scientific hypotheses in the following respects.

1 Just as the scientific hypothesis that life is not created but rather the result of natural processes leads to attempts to duplicate the 'primordial soup' in the laboratory, and thereby to 'create life in the test-tube,' so do rights-claims lead to attempts to have these rights embodied in a legal system.[3]

2 Just as the attempts to create life in the test-tube lead to success or failure and thus confirm, or disconfirm, the scientific hypothesis, so the attempts to embody rights of persons into legal systems lead to success or failure. And, in the case of success, they lead to the possibility of examining whether the resulting conditions of life are indeed the desired ones. Both failure and the discovery that the outcome of success is not as foreseen and desired are reasons to reject or revise a rights-claim, whereas success in both senses tends to make the rights-claim a more firmly held moral belief.

3 Later we shall see that just as a scientific hypothesis is part of a larger theory which is at stake in the outcome of the experiment, so rights-claims are part of a larger doctrine (the liberal tradition) which is at stake when rights-claims are examined in the light of historical experience.

Since rights-claims are intended to move groups of people to political action, we shall ask whether large numbers of people will understand a given rights-claim in the same way and thus be moved to concerted action. Analogously, we demand of a scientific hypothesis that it be sufficiently clear to produce agreement on what would count as confirming evidence.

In this paper, I am concerned to examine not arguments in

---

1 It is possible to deny that rights-claims are value-judgments. That does not matter for the following discussion. What matters is that they can be viewed in the light in which I propose to view them. It is also possible to hold different views with respect to different categories of value-judgments. The latter possibility need not be considered in this context, although I do not intend to dismiss it.

2 Elaborated in many of his works.

3 We need not distinguish here between additions to an existing legal code by means sanctioned by that code, and political or social revolutions bringing in their train a new legal system.

favor of the doctrine of rights of persons, but rather critical arguments against the doctrine. It should be said, however, whatever the arguments, that those who wish to continue to couch their political aspirations and their criticism of existing social relations in the language of rights can point to considerable historical evidence in their favor. One cannot deny that the doctrine of rights of persons, and the liberal tradition of which it forms a part, have proved to be remarkably *effective* for three centuries.[1] Let us consider this briefly.

The political doctrine of the liberal tradition expressed the aspirations of the rising bourgeoisie, justified their revolutionary activities in their own eyes, and to some extent in the eyes of others, and asserted in general terms precisely those rights of persons which are made precise and enforceable in the legal systems which developed from the middle of the seventeenth century in English-speaking countries and ultimately in most parts of the world. These changes both reflected changing economic relationships and were in the interest of those who held and propagated the liberal tradition.

When one examines the doctrine of rights of persons with this success in mind, it becomes apparent that three rights played a central role: the right to property, the right to equality before the law, and the right to equal participation in the political process. Of these, the right to property proved to be the clearest, least ambiguous and least controversial. Except for the question of slave-owning, to which we shall return, there was in general no disagreement on how one acquired property justly, what one was entitled to do with one's property, and under what carefully circumscribed conditions the state was entitled to a portion of one's property. That that agreement no longer exists, even among persons who clearly adhere to the liberal tradition, does not contradict this claim, although it suggests that the time for re-examination has come.

The right to equality before the law, as understood in Locke's time, was also uncontentious. What strikes one in retrospect as

1 By the liberal tradition I mean here not all of the democratic tradition – in particular, I do not mean the form which that tradition takes in Rousseau, and which may be said to be carried further in Marxism. Rather I mean the tradition as it is found in Locke, foreshadowed in Hobbes, developed further by J. S. Mill, and most recently restated by John Rawls. The essence of that tradition is captured by Rawls when he insists on the priority of equal liberties but believes this to be compatible with inequalities with respect to other primary goods (*A Theory of Justice*, Cambridge, Mass., 1971, p. 302).

curious are the kinds of laws with respect to which all persons were regarded as equal, and the kinds of laws with respect to which they were not regarded as equals. It was not only with respect to political rights that women, Jews in England, blacks in the United States, and the propertyless were not equals. To mention but one example, women did not enjoy the same property rights, nor the same rights to enter into contracts, as men. As already suggested, that situation is perhaps best described by saying that not all human beings were regarded as persons, or as full persons, and therefore were not held to have all the rights of persons.[1]

When we turn to the issue of equal political rights (the right to vote and the right to seek public office), it is apparent that no agreement existed even in the seventeenth century. The Levellers did not advocate universal male suffrage but they did believe that a much larger number of males were entitled to equal political rights. One may be tempted to point to this disagreement as evidence for saying that rights-claims, or at any rate this rights-claim, was not sufficiently unambiguous, or not sufficiently clear, to produce concerted action. It seems to me that history does not support this contention. The disagreement between the Levellers and the other opponents of absolutistic or aristocratic government did not prevent effective political action, and the Leveller's view and finally the universal male suffrage view prevailed in the fullness of time.

That a certain amount of confusion need not be an obstacle to effective political action is also illustrated by the example of the Civil Rights Movement in the 1950s and early 1960s in the United States. That movement involved many individuals and it brought about legal and to a lesser extent social and attitudinal changes. At the same time, the arguments presented to the public by proponents of the Civil Rights Movement involved what might be considered a hopeless confusion between legal and constitutional rights on the one hand and rights of persons on the other. The movement was directed primarily by the claim that certain specific forms of racial discrimination were unconstitutional. Such a claim always lacks legal status in the beginning. Indeed, of school segregation the claim was in fact a challenge to a previous determination of the constitutionality of 'separate but equal'

---

1 Of course, I am not suggesting that a peculiar view (from our perspective) of personhood caused these legal inequalities; I am suggesting that a peculiar view of personhood served to justify these inequalities on the ideological level.

schools. The plaintiffs were really saying that a certain institution *should* be declared unconstitutional because it violated rights of persons. As it developed, of course the Civil Rights Movement became more militant. It not only fought in the courts but used various tactics of civil disobedience. We shall discuss the later phase below.

Nevertheless, intellectual confusion is not a recommendation. The first sustained philosophical criticism of the doctrine of rights of persons, the criticism due to the legal positivists, was concerned precisely with confusion. The criticism arose from within the liberal tradition and must be taken seriously.

The essential point which the legal positivists were concerned to establish is summarized by Hart:[1]

> What these thinkers were, in the main, concerned to promote was clarity and honesty in the formulation of the theoretical and moral issues raised by the existence of particular laws which were morally iniquitous but were enacted in proper form, clear in meaning, and satisfied all the acknowledged criteria of validity of a system. Their view was that, in thinking about such laws, both the theorist and the unfortunate official or private citizen who was called on to apply or obey them, could only be confused by an invitation to refuse the title of 'law' or 'valid' to them. They thought that, to confront these problems, more candid resources were available, which would bring into focus far better, every relevant intellectual and moral consideration we should say, 'This is law; but it is too iniquitous to be applied or obeyed'.

Hart does not deny all content to Natural Law doctrine. Rather he seems to feel that in its clear and non-confusing content it does not go far enough. When he objected to the doctrine of Natural Rights as a less than honest way of dealing with the question of how to justify punishing Germans accused of 'crimes against humanity', he had, I believe, a valid point. To attempt to justify a *judicial* procedure by way of a concept so easily confused with a *juridical* concept was indeed confusing. The issue was not whether rights of persons had been violated by the accused – of course they had been – but on what basis a court of law existing essentially through superior force of arms could punish individuals who had obeyed the law of the land. It was Hart's position that legalistic language served only to cover up what was essentially a

1 H. L. A. Hart, *The Concept of Law*, Oxford, 1961, p. 203.

moral question. Both the war criminal and those who set up the war crimes tribunal were faced with moral choices. The war criminal evaded the moral choice by claiming that he obeyed the positive law. The Natural Law defenders of the tribunal hid their moral choice in legal-sounding terminology.

The fact that in some situations appeal to the rights of persons is inappropriate or confusing or dishonest does not militate against all appeals to the rights of persons. Especially when, as in the case of the Civil Rights Movement, the intention of those who put forward a rights-claim is that the right in question be embodied in a legal code, the 'confusion' between moral and juridical notions is at worst a surface confusion, and does not hide any moral issue.

It is to be noticed that the theory of political obligation and sovereignty adopted by the legal positivist leads one to reject the concept of a right to revolution. For, if we take appeals to rights of persons as demands that these rights be embodied in a legal code, then it is clear that there cannot be in this sense a right to revolution. Such a right cannot be embodied in a legal code, just as a legal code cannot include a law that it be obeyed. If one were to say that persons, or rather a class of persons, or a people, have the right to revolution, one would be saying only that they do no moral wrong if they revolt, although in the course of the revolution they would undoubtedly do many legal wrongs. But unless one specifies clearly the conditions for revolution, for example by specifying which rights of persons cannot be systematically denied without justifying revolt, the claim seems indefensible. On the other hand, the specification of specific rights of persons asserts *inter alia* that defending these specific rights even by force is to do no wrong.[1] Here again, it might be said, moral issues are hidden. For if persons *qua* persons have certain rights, and if it is therefore not wrong to defend these rights, it may nevertheless be wrong to defend them by means of tactics which violate the rights of other persons. The Civil Rights Movement in its later phase of non-violent civil disobedience may be said to have been clearly aware of precisely this problem. During that phase certain positive laws were systematically violated, and insofar as these laws protected or

1 This last point was perhaps seen most clearly by Hobbes. Hobbes was concerned to deny that 'subjects' have rights against the 'sovereign' precisely because he saw the doctrine of rights as an invitation to rebellion. At the same time he recognized one natural right, the right to life, and he argued quite consistently that therefore one was entitled to defend one's life against the sovereign, however justly (i.e. legally) one might have been condemned to death.

guaranteed certain legal rights of individuals, these legal rights were also violated. However, it is not difficult to see in the non-violence and in the non-destructiveness of that movement a concern for rights of persons. Once again, one can say at most that the language was confused. One cannot say, as in the case of the war criminals, that the confused language prevented the development of a clear strategy or an awareness of moral issues.

The conclusion at which one should arrive seems to me to be this. The moral issues with which advocates of rights of persons seek to deal are complex. Some of these issues are more felicitously dealt with in different terms. Moreover, it may be the case that all of these issues can be dealt with in other terms. Above all, legal positivism has not produced any argument against the moral beliefs which we are accustomed to find expressed in the doctrine of rights of persons. So far, no evidence has been adduced that these moral beliefs are false. Let us therefore take a new look at rights of persons.

It seems to me that of all rights of persons ever claimed by anyone, the right to life plays a particularly key role. It is the only natural right recognized by Hobbes; it forms the basis for Locke's intricate argument concerning the natural (i.e. pre-contractual) right to property; even authors who tend not to speak of rights find in human vulnerability the prime reason for social organization under a rule of law.[1] At the same time, an important concern of political philosophers has been to justify the death penalty and the sending of citizens into battle. In both cases, the right of the state to take a human life is based immediately on the obligation of the state to preserve the lives of its citizens and thus ultimately on their right to life. On the other hand, arguments against the death penalty and against conscription also claim that persons have the right to live. Although arguments against the death penalty tend to be intricate and complex, they generally intend to show either that the death penalty cannot be justified in terms of its deterrent consequences, or that the right to life cannot be forfeit by any crime, even that of willful murder. Both these arguments take the right to life seriously. Similarly, those who argue against conscription, although they argue immediately in terms of freedom of conscience, raise the issue of whether it is ever, or in a particular war, justified to take human lives, or whether it is right to take the lives of members of the enemy population in a particular manner. Some objected to serving in the US Armed Forces in the war in

1 Hart, op. cit., ch. 9.

Vietnam because civilians were killed in large numbers and killed in a particularly horrible manner. Others objected because they felt that the war was unjust, that the aims to be accomplished if the United States were to win were not aims which justified the killing of anyone. Still others objected on the general pacifist ground that it is always wrong to kill a human being, or that the organized killing which is called 'war' is always wrong. All these reasons recognize the right to life as a more or less stringent, more or less indefeasible, right.

A few additional remarks will complete the picture which I am trying to present. It seems at first sight that the right to life is the basic right. If one has lost that right one has no rights at all. If the state or another individual may kill one without doing wrong, then surely the state or the individual may deprive one of any other right without doing wrong: keep one as a slave or take one's property. Not everyone will agree with the spirit of this analysis, and perhaps no one will agree with it completely. It seems to many morally sensitive persons that even the condemned criminal is entitled to be treated with as much dignity as is compatible with preventing his escape while he is awaiting execution. It seems to most morally sensitive persons that the death penalty should be administered in as painless a fashion as possible. One may be willing to grant that under certain circumstances a captured enemy may be shot but deny that he may be tortured in order to extract information. It may then seem that there is a right which is even more fundamental, even less alienable, than the right to life. One is tempted to call it the right to remain a person as long as one lives. Actually, what is involved here is not appropriately called a right. Rather, it is a conception of human dignity without which the concept of rights of persons cannot even arise.

Still, the right to life has been far from unqualified. The right to property has played, or plays, a large role. Locke argued that a military commander could execute a soldier who refused to obey orders, but could not deprive him of his money.[1] Others have argued against taxing the rich to feed the poor. For many centuries the death penalty seemed an appropriate penalty for theft, even thefts committed without any threat to the life of the victim. Even today, policemen who shoot and kill thieves, or would-be thieves, running from the scene of the crime, are acquitted of any legal wrong-doing.

1 John Locke, *The Second Treatise of Government*, ed. Thomas P. Peardon (New York, 1952), paragraph 139.

In summary, there is a widespread moral belief, indeed what I am inclined to call a moral fact, which can be expressed by saying that persons have a right to live, but this moral fact is extremely complex and stands in complicated relations with other moral facts. There is relatively little agreement on the details of this fact and its relation to other facts. Thus for Hobbes the right to life meant the right to self-defense and indeed was an inalienable right. For most philosophers it is both more and less than that. It is more in the sense that certain definite obligations on the part of the state, and to some extent on the part of other individuals, follow from the right to life. It is less because it is merely a *prima facie* right, a right which can be overridden or forfeited. To say that it is a *prima facie* right is to say that a moral justification must be given when the right is violated but no moral justification needs to be given when it is honored. Disagreement arises over the question of what is to count as a moral justification for taking a human life, for placing a human life in unusual jeopardy. There may be disagreement over what is to count as 'unusual jeopardy.' In the last category there are the debates over health and safety regulations in factories and mines.

This suggests that rights-claims are very complex moral claims expressed in very simple language, and that the simplicity of the language tends to hide the complexity of the claims. This impression is reinforced by the fact that there is no agreement even on the primacy of the right to life. Thus Hart defends the thesis that if there are any moral rights at all then there must be at least one natural right, 'the equal right of all men to be free,'[1] of which he says that it is all that the liberal tradition needs. This right is for him not absolute, indefeasible or imprescriptible, and he recognizes that it is vacuous unless some restrictions are placed on what counts as a moral justification for interference.

Once again one is tempted to conclude that it would be better not to talk about rights of persons at all. The possibilities for misunderstanding and disagreement seem endless, and one is inclined to think that clearer and less ambiguous language can be found. But the latter seems to me to be an illusion. It seems to me to be characteristic of all political debate couched in moral terms (and perhaps of all moral argument) that conflicting moral claims can be put forward using the same sort of terminology. Also, conflicting conclusions can be drawn from the same moral

[1] H. L. A. Hart, 'Are there any Natural Rights?', *Philosophical Review*, vol. 64, 1955, pp. 175–91.

premise because (a) in general the conclusion requires more than one premise, and (b) when there are irreconcilable conflicts of interest, they will find their expression in conflicting interpretations and applications of the same general principle.

What one should conclude from the preceding discussion is not that rights-claims should be eschewed; but that rights-claims are context-dependent in two ways. First, we cannot assume that the right to liberty of which Locke spoke is the same right as the equal right of all men to be free of which Hart speaks. Indeed, one can produce a convincing argument for the claim that liberty meant freedom of religion for the seventeenth-century Englishman and freedom from feudal restrictions for the eighteenth-century Frenchman. Second, we cannot assume that the same list of rights, however reinterpreted in the light of changing social circumstances, will serve to express the aspirations of all oppressed classes.

Recognizing this double context-dependency involves a denial of an essential element of the original doctrine. For whether the rights of persons in the liberal doctrine are said to be self-evident, or a necessary presupposition of any moral critique of social and political arrangements, or conclusions from more or less utilitarian premises, these rights are none the less said to be rights of persons *qua* persons, independent of any particular social context, timeless, and not a matter of class. If this were so, one could use the same terminology of rights to express one's aspirations for a socialist society, and to justify one's opposition to deep-rooted features of capitalism. One would simply have to modify the original list by addition, excision, and re-interpretation. This has been the method of advocates of reform, the method of those who agree that the doctrine of rights of persons is essentially sound in its claim to timelessness and universality, but grant that in specifics it suffers from the provincialism of its original proponents. (I call them advocates of reform not to indicate their distaste for revolution. The point is that they see the ideology as requiring reform rather than discarding.)

In this manner freedom of speech, certain freedoms of association, universal suffrage, the abolition of property qualifications for holders of elective office, and so on were introduced into the liberal tradition. The right of self-determination of nations, and the equal rights movements of our own day may be seen as further elaborations of the same ideology. But elaboration clearly has its limitations.

There is a continual risk that the new rights claimed will come in conflict with older rights. This is most clearly seen precisely in those cases where, so to speak, the criterion of being a person is widened. Consider, for example, the debate over the abolition of slavery. We may say that the abolitionists held that blacks were persons at least to the extent that they were entitled to enjoy the basics of liberty. But, for the slave-owner, abolition represented an infringement of his property rights. Similarly, what are called in the United States Affirmative Action Programs, programs designed to insure the admission of minorities and women to jobs and institutions of higher learning, are seen by some as an infringement of the rights of the owners of the relevant businesses, or of the rights of the schools, and in some cases as an infringement of the rights even of the white male applicants. Yet one can argue with propriety within the context of the liberal ideology that such programs are an attempt to insure that blacks and women enjoy equal rights (or the right to equal opportunity) in the face of widespread prejudice. This is not really surprising. Any person's right provides a moral justification for limiting the freedom of another, as Hart points out. But, as he also points out, my having the right to be free entails that others may not coerce or restrain me except from acts which would in turn coerce or restrain others.[1] As the list of rights embodied into law grows, each particular right tends to become more limited, and the state is provided with a legal justification, based on a prior moral justification, for limiting freedoms seen as restrictive of the freedoms of others. Unless rights of persons become so embodied in law, they are essentially of little value. A major point in asserting rights of persons is, after all, to advocate their incorporation into law.

It is thus not surprising that precisely to the extent that the liberal tradition becomes more liberal, so to speak, it loses its moral force. There is less unanimity on what are rights of persons, there is less agreement on the extent of even those rights on which there is agreement, conflicts of rights become more frequent, and, in the absence of an agreed-upon and fixed order of precedence, such conflicts are essentially unresolvable within the confines of a doctrine of rights.

In any case, reform of the kind so far discussed will not lead to a list of rights which would express the aspirations and criticisms of socialists. Of course Marx, and Marxists in general, have not

---

1 'Are there any Natural Rights?', *passim*.

tried to do so. Nor, it seems to me, can they do so. It will be instructive to note some particular points of difficulty. They will lead to a major contention of this essay.

The abolitionist could find a place in the liberal tradition by pointing out that blacks are persons, appealing to one right (the right to liberty) in order to justify limiting another (the right to property). The socialist wants to abolish all private property in (major) means of production. But to what right of persons can he appeal in order to justify such a drastic limitation of so fundamental a right? What he must challenge is a web of interconnected concepts and empirical assumptions. But that is to say that he must challenge the whole liberal tradition.

Again, the liberal tradition views the state as a protector of rights, and hence the state as a good: the theory is simultaneously a theory of political obligation. But the socialist regards the state as an instrument of class oppression. His ultimate aim is a society of abundance in which there are no classes and no state. If he were to speak of rights, his intent would be quite incompatible with the intentions of the liberal tradition. His basic theory of persons and of society is incompatible with the theory which underlies the liberal tradition.

Perhaps this is seen most clearly when one considers the theory of alienation found in the writings of the young Marx. Could one add to the traditional list of rights, or could one substitute for parts or all of that list, the right not to be alienated? The suggestion is absurd. Rights are the prized possessions of alienated persons.

We said at the beginning that it is instructive to regard rights-claims as analogous to scientific hypotheses. Rights-claims suggest and justify certain courses of action, they lead to predictions concerning the structure of a future society and the quality of life in that society. Scientific hypotheses often lead to large numbers of true predicitions, and then they fail. Such failures force one to re-examine the whole theory of which the particular hypothesis is a part. That, it seems to me, is precisely the position in which we find ourselves with respect to the liberal tradition. Let us, therefore, look at that tradition as a whole.

The theory asserts that each adult person is a self-contained individual, 'an isolated monad withdrawn into himself,' whose liberty is 'not founded upon the relations between man and man, but rather upon the separation of man from man,' whose right of property is 'the right of self-interest. . . . It leads every man to see in other men not the *realization* but rather the *limitation* of his own liberty.' 'The only bond between men is natural necessity, need and private interest, the preservation of their property and their egoistic persons.'[1] This summary of one basic assumption of the liberal tradition is due to Marx, and the assumption is indeed, as Macpherson called it, a theory of 'possessive individualism.'[2] Locke, Hobbes and Bentham all would have agreed that the isolated individual is, so to speak, all we have to work with, that persons confront each other as adversaries vying for their share of scarce goods. The fact that Locke maintains that even in the 'state of nature' persons are subject to moral laws does not contradict this claim, for the moral laws are precisely the rules within the confines of which the war of each against each is to be conducted. Least of all does it matter whether the view is coupled with a social doctrine or not, although we shall see that a social contract is peculiarly fitting in this context.

The question which concerns us is whether this basic assumption is true. Quite clearly it reflects the relationship which holds between two members of the bourgeoisie, or persons who aspire to rise into the bourgeoisie. From the point of view of someone who aspires to a bigger slice of the pie, the size and nature of the pie is only indirectly relevant. Contrary to Hume it is true that even in a state of great abundance, competition for what Hobbes called 'glory,' for profits, power and control, might well be the dominating motives of the egoistic man. But even if that were not so, we are not living in a world of abundance. Moreover, this is an assumption which the bourgeois, or the aspiring bourgeois, wishes to be believed by everyone. He must, on the one hand, break down the limits which feudal or semi-feudal notions of cast, guild or station put on competition and on access to political power. More importantly, he must prevent workers and peasants from conceiving of a class interest which overrides or transcends the interest of any one individual. From the point of view of the rising bourgeoisie, we have argued, and also from the point of view of the bourgeoisie in power, the assumption that individuals confront each other as adversaries, constrained only by rules which are 'fair' in the sense that they do not give an advantage to anyone, over and above the advantages which he may already have, is an assumption which is true.

1 Karl Marx, *Early Writings*, translated and edited by T. B. Bottomore (New York, 1963), pp. 24–6.
2 C. B. Macpherson, *The Political Theory of Possessive Individualism* (Oxford, 1962).

But from a broader perspective the assumption is false. Viewed as a prediction of the organization of society, it suggests that human beings, regardless of changes in the material conditions of life, will always face each other as competitors, will never be in a position to replace what is at best civilized enmity by love, trust or friendship. If that were so, then there would be indeed no point in a socialist revolution, since sooner or later, whatever precarious unity existed during the revolutionary period, individual would once again strive against individual and a new ruling class would emerge. Moreover, if every individual is indeed egoistic, if the common interest is never more than the sum of the interests of everyone involved, if each individual forms his own idea of the good for himself without reference to the good of anyone else, with the possible exception of family and close friends, then it is not unreasonable to believe that one can further one's own prospects better and more effectively by concentrating one's efforts precisely on one's own prospects.

In fact human beings are capable of viewing each other in a different light. Class struggle is not a figment of the Marxist imagination, a fact which the bourgeois knows as well as the proletarian. It is in the interest of the bourgeois to hide this fact, since he needs class-consciousness and class-solidarity only as a response to the class-consciousness and class-solidarity of the worker. For the worker, however, class-solidarity must be seen as the *sine qua non* of success, whether his aim is reform or social revolution. The reason for this will become apparent when we examine a second basic assumption of the liberal tradition, the assumption of equality.

Before we examine that assumption, I wish to raise a further objection to the 'isolated monad' assumption. In a world as populated as ours, and with a technology as complex as ours, no individual is self-sufficient. That, of course, is a truism. But the alienated, egoistic man is not supposed to be self-sufficient in such a radical sense; to raise this as an objection would be gratuitous. The early stages of Locke's argument concerning property do indeed presuppose such a self-sufficiency and also an abundance, an abundance not of goods but of the possibilities to create goods in a self-sufficient manner. But in the later stages of his argument, and in the real world of capitalism, a given individual is self-sufficient only when he extends his labor power by the purchase of that of another.

When Locke says that 'the turf my servant has cut . . . becomes(s) my property'[1] or when the corporate owners of an industrial enterprise say that the goods produced by their employers are theirs, the isolated monad is not a single human being, nor a 'legal person' in the sense in which a corporation is a legal person. The isolated monad is rather like an organism constituted of more than one (often very many) human beings, of which one person, natural or legal, is the head (or brain, or mind). But that, it seems to me, introduces a fundamental incoherence into the basic assumption. The very theory which glorifies the individual *qua* individual is conducive to the development of a society in which almost no one is an individual. The interest of the company, for the sake of which the worker is supposed to work harder or forego a rise, for the sake of which the executive is supposed to become an 'organization man', is in no intelligible sense the sum of the interests of all those who 'belong' to the company. In this sense, then, the isolated monad assumption, which is an essential part of the liberal tradition, is false. Of course, it would be wrong to say that the liberal ideology is single-handedly responsible for the related historical developments. The liberal ideology did not produce capitalism; but the liberal ideology for all its ultimate incoherence served well to anticipate, justify and make 'natural' the social and legal changes required for the full flourishing of capitalism. However, the very development of capitalism has made evident the particular incoherence just noticed.

A second basic assumption of the liberal ideology is the assumption of the equality of all persons. In his very illuminating article, The Two Democratic Traditions', Sabine says[2]

> there have been two democratic traditions, or at least two distinguishable strands in the democratic tradition; . . . one has been more characteristically Anglo-American and the other more characteristically French; . . . the first gave primary importance to liberty while the second gave primary importance to equality.

What I have called 'the liberal tradition' is what he calls 'the Anglo-American democratic tradition.' But while he seems to me quite correct in his characterization, the liberal tradition does contain, not indeed as an ideal aspired to but as a fundamental assumption, an assumption of equality. In its earliest appearance, it must be admitted, equality in the sense of equality before the

1 Op. cit., paragraph 28.
2 George H. Sabine, 'The Two Democratic Traditions', *Philosophical Review*, vol. 61, 1952.

law was not merely an assumption but an ideal. But, as said above, equality as an ideal or as an expression of aspirations to be realized is always closely tied to the idea of equal rights, which is to say liberties. In defence of the claim to equal rights, there is the assumption of equality. It is difficult to see, however, precisely what this equality amounts to.

In Hobbes and Locke it amounts to the claim that no human being is so naturally superior to another (in mind or body) that he can base his claim to power on that superiority alone.[1] But that assumption by itself does not lead anywhere. Or rather, it may lead everywhere. Coupled with other assumptions it can serve as a premise in an argument for one-man rule (Hobbes), class rule (Locke), or universal suffrage. To the extent that equality of persons entails that *ab initio* persons have equal rights, the assumption leads rather naturally into a social-contract doctrine, for the social contract involves a trade-off of rights, whether the contract be Hobbesian, Lockean or Rawlsian. But this does not help us here. We cannot justify the assumption of equality by claiming equal rights, for we are now examining the total doctrine of which rights-claims are a part. What then is the particular equality of persons which is needed as an assumption in the liberal tradition and which goes beyond a rough equality in mind and body?[2] Macpherson suggests in interpretation of this equality that all persons are equally subject to the law of the market in what he calls a 'competitive market society'.[3] I agree with Macpherson's interpretation provided that the assumption is understood as asserting that all persons confront each other on essentially equal terms, i.e. with comparable advantages and disadvantages, in competition and bargaining. That assumption, it seems to me, is most clearly evident in Bentham. It seems to me, further, that one could make a case for that assumption if both of the following

1 It is perhaps not out of place to note in this connection that the most dangerous attacks on rights of persons, or on egalitarianism such as it is, are based on claims that certain kinds of persons are not equal to others in precisely this sense. Slavery has almost always been justified by the claim that the slaves were barbarians; Jews were said to be inferior in mind if not in body by Hitler's scientists; Jensen and his cohorts in the United States oppose demands for equal opportunity by attempting to 'prove' the genetic inferiority of blacks.

2 That equality in mind and body is a necessary presupposition of the liberal tradition is not denied here (see note 1). Nor is it denied that coupled with the first assumption – the assumption of the 'isolated monad' – it will lead to some claims for equal rights. The point here is that that assumption is not sufficient for the liberal tradition.

3 Op. cit. p. 85.

were the case: (a) that what human beings are trading, what they bargain and compete for, is always the product of their labor, not their labor-power, and (b) that persons are free to choose on the basis of a rational calculation of their own best interest what they are to produce. For just as capital in the perfectly competitive economy moves into sectors where profits are highest, until profits become again equalized, so persons would choose to produce what they can trade most advantageously, resulting in equal advantages for all. Clearly, the functioning of this competitive society, indeed its continued existence as a competitive society, depends on maximal freedom to choose one's own way of life, maximal freedom to compete, the absence of force and coercion, which would prevent one from realizing one's advantages, and full access to all relevant information. In short, it depends on fair rules in the sense mentioned above.

One may argue that in a pre-industrial society this state of affairs could indeed obtain, although of course it did not. But in a highly industrial society, whether organized on capitalist or socialist principles, it cannot obtain, because of the nature of the means of production and therefore the manner in which goods are produced. What most human beings are trading is not the product of their labor but their labor-power, for unless someone buys their labor-power, they cannot produce anything. They do not own means of production. Nor can they, as producers, determine what they are to produce – i.e. what it would be most advantageous for them to produce. What is to be produced is determined by those who own or control the means of production, and only to a very limited extent can the producer, not *qua* producer but *qua* consumer, influence that decision. We should all prefer butter to guns, but we can influence only (and only to a limited extent) the kind of 'butter' to be produced, and we have essentially no voice in determining how much 'butter' versus how many 'guns.' What one wants among other things, if one wants socialism, is that human needs, not capitalist profits, should determine what is to be produced. But because of the nature of the productive forces, this cannot be achieved by a 'return' to a perfect competitive market society which never was. Thus the assumption of equality, as we find it in the liberal tradition, turns out to be a false assumption.

All of this, of course, is not to say that persons are not equal or should not be treated as equals. However, equality is always equality in some respect. For when one demands equality for women, for example, one is saying that the obvious biological differences between men and women are to be ignored in a specific context, e.g. when it comes to voting, or when it comes to doing housework. The equality-assumption of the liberal tradition is that the obvious inequality between the owner of the means of production (or, rather the buyer of labor-power), and the person who has nothing but his labor-power to sell, is to be ignored (it was claimed not to exist). When labor refused to ignore it by organizing unions, when workers ceased to see themselves as 'egoistic' persons, and ceased to that extent to be 'egoistic' persons (thus falsifying the first assumption of the liberal tradition), labor was accused precisely of upsetting this spurious equality. At the same time, workers were given the right to vote, given a spurious political equality – here I use 'political' in the narrowest sense – in place of the real equality in the market place to which they aspired.

We have said that the equality-assumption of the liberal tradition is false. We have also said that in a socialist society people will be equal. We must give this claim of equality a new sense. That new sense involves both a radical rejection of the real inequalities suffered by persons because of their sex, race, religion or class, and an affirmation of the equal dignity of persons not as 'isolated monads' but as 'species-beings.'[1] For us, so deeply steeped in the liberal tradition, that is a difficult conception. Before I try to elucidate it, let me say something about the sense in which the inequalities of sex, race, religion and class will be eliminated. There will be no classes, and one may presume that there will be no religion, at any rate in the form in which we now know it, not because it will be suppressed from above, but because it will lack any basis in the reality of person's lives. We cannot foresee a disappearance of races, at any rate for many centuries. Sexual differences in the biological sense are a fact of nature.

But facts of nature can be seen in different ways, and in a sense they can be not seen. Just as it is absurd in physics to consider relativistic complications when one deals with middlesized low-energy processes, so it will become absurd to consider differences in sex in all contexts but the one where it is biologically relevant. But that, it seems to me, will happen only to the extent that individuals view themselves not as isolated monads but as species-beings. By way of a contemporary analogy, if one's car is stalled in the middle of the road, one does not consider the skin color of the passer-by who helps to push it out of the way. For that short span

1 Marx, op. cit., p. 31.

of time there are two persons with a common purpose. The relationship is not one of trading advantages, or competitors, or adversaries. There is for that span of time an unspoken trust. Note by the way, how inappropriate it would be to speak here of rights. I do not claim a right to have you help me push and you do not claim a right to help me.

What I am suggesting, then, is that the liberal assumption of equality is false. But that is not to be taken as a simple critique of capitalist society, as if one were to say: in present-day capitalist society the equality of which the liberal tradition speaks is not realized, but it could and should be realized in another society. The equality of which the liberal tradition speaks is inextricably connected with the individualism of the liberal tradition and we cannot have the one without the other. A comparison with scientific theories is again instructive. The *concept* of mass is different in relativity theory and Newtonian mechanics. Relativity theory does not replace pieces of Newtonian physics and leave other parts intact. The Marxist view of man and society is not a replacing of pieces of the liberal tradition, leaving other parts intact.[1] The *concept* of equality is a different concept. Although I cannot spell out in detail what that concept of equality entails – that would require another essay – I should like to suggest that it is the equality appropriate to persons with a common purpose, and committed to realizing that purpose. It is a purpose which the young Marx described as human emancipation, and which one might, in view of what I said earlier, describe as the realization of human dignity.

I should like to say now what I have *not* done in this essay. I

1 It would take us too far into the philosophy of science to pursue this line of thought. However, I wish to point out some reasons why the analogy is worth pursuing. Just as Newtonian mechanics is the correct theory for dealing with middle-sized, low-energy phenomena, so the liberal tradition was the correct theory for the rising bourgeoisie for dealing both with the dying aristocracy and with the rising proletariat. Even more it was the correct theory (or at any rate a correct theory) for dealing with a certain period in the technological history of mankind. In inanimate nature we simultaneously find different types of phenomena, best dealt with by different theories; in human society we find a succession of stages for which different theories are appropriate. Different scientific theories may use the same words, and philosophers of science are not agreed on whether these words have the same meaning, or whether they refer to the same real entity, or indeed whether they refer at all. Unlike 'rights', 'equality' has its place, I think, in both the liberal tradition and in Marxist theory. It clearly does not have the same meaning, but I am inclined to think that there is a moral fact to which it refers, just as I believe that there is a real entity to which 'mass' refers.

have not examined the liberal tradition and the doctrine of rights of persons from inside. If I had wished to do that, I should have examined it in its most fully developed modern version – that one presented by Rawls.[1] Secondly, I have not presented *the* Marxist critique of the liberal tradition. If I had wished to do that I should have examined in detail what Marx, Engels and other Marxists have said concerning the liberal ideology.

What I have done is to examine the hypothesis that persons *qua* persons have rights, and the liberal tradition of which that hypothesis is a part. I have examined this theory of persons and of society in the manner in which I, as a philosopher of science, believe that any theory should be examined. I have asked whether the theory is sufficiently clear to be tested, and whether the theory is true. I have concluded that the theory is clear enough to be tested, and I have concluded that it is not true, despite the fact that it was nearly enough true of the social conditions of an earlier period to play an important role. However, a theory of persons and society is not merely a descriptive, explanatory and predictive theory. It also expresses the aspirations for society of those who believe it to be true. If such a theory is widely believed to be true, that fact itself becomes a causal factor influencing the subsequent course of history. Needless to say, the result may not be what the theory predicts.

Because a political theory, or rather the belief in such a theory, itself becomes a causal factor in human history, and because the critic too has his or her own aspirations for society, these aspirations will influence the form and content of the critique. While it seems to me that the method used in this paper is one which persons of widely different political persuasions could use profitably, and while I believe that it can be used with respect to many different political theories, persons who do not share the Marxist perspective of the present writer will undoubtedly come to somewhat different conclusions.[2]

1　John Rawls, op. cit.
2　This too has its analogue in the critique of scientific theories. A scientific theory is not abandoned simply because some contrary evidence is produced. It is abandoned only when there is a better theory to take its place, and there is often room for disagreement concerning the next theory.
Scientists must be persuaded to take a given candidate-theory seriously enough to subject it to further tests. Just so, in politics, many persons must be persuaded to share the new aspirations in order that the new theory will be tested in the arena of political action.

6 The Theory of the Collapse of Capitalism

LUCIO COLLETTI

Marx's attitude towards capitalism is a function of two different perspectives. The first is the *revolutionary* perspective, which aims at the overthrow of bourgeois society in order to re-establish on a new basis the human relationships which have been reversed and turned 'upside down' in this society. The second is the *scientific* perspective, which aims at theoretically reconstructing the way the system functions and develops. Although quite different, these two perspectives are not set apart in Marx's work. Rather, they are so connected that each is supported and reinforced by the fact that it follows as a consequence of the other. The revolutionary perspective derives its strength from the fact that it arises as a consequence of scientific analysis, and the analysis is pushed to its extreme conclusions by the orientation and impulse of revolutionary teleology.

These features of Marx's thought can be grasped in general outline by briefly examining his critique of utopian socialism and then integrating this critique with the one developed against the major classical political economists. When we have considered these matters, we will pass on specifically to the theory of the collapse of capitalism.

Marx primarily stresses the fact that utopian socialism opposes modern bourgeois society by taking up a 'moralistic' viewpoint, an abstract and subjective viewpoint. It denounces the system's 'injustices' without, however, understanding its real mechanisms from within. Its condemnation proceeds from ideals and criteria lacking foundation in the reality being criticized. In the words of Engels,[1]

> the Utopians attempted to evolve [the solution of social problems] out of the human brain. Society presented nothing but wrongs: to remove these was the task of reason. It was necessary, then, to discover a new and more perfect system of social order

1 Frederick Engels, 'Socialism: Utopian and Scientific', in Karl Marx and Frederick Engels, *Selected Works* (Moscow, 1962), vol. II, p. 121.

III

and to impose this upon society from without by propaganda, and wherever it was possible, by the example of model experiments. These new social systems were foredoomed as utopian; the more completely they were worked out in detail, the more they could not avoid drifting off into pure fantasies.

Naturally, the immaturity of this early type of socialism must itself be considered a product of the objective situation.[1]

The utopians . . . were utopians because they could be nothing else at a time when capitalist production was as yet so little developed. They necessarily had to construct the elements of a new society out of their own heads, because within the old society the elements of the new were not as yet generally apparent.

Engels stresses the profound innovation made in this field by historical materialism: it provided a radically different critique of bourgeois society. This critique was not a matter of opposing abstract ideals to existing reality.[2]

The means of getting rid of the incongruities that have been brought to light must also be present, in a more or less developed condition, within the changed modes of production themselves. These means are not to be *invented*, spun out of the head, but *discovered* with the aid of the head in the existing material facts of production.

This new program is executed in Marx's *Capital*, compared to which utopian socialism's limitations stand out clearly. In fact, writes Lenin, in criticizing capitalist society, the old socialism[3]

condemned and damned it, it dreamed of its destruction, it had visions of a better order and endeavored to convince the rich of the immorality of exploitation. But . . . [it] could not indicate the real solution. It could not explain the real nature of wage-slavery under capitalism. It could not reveal the laws of capitalist development or show what *social force* is capable of becoming the creator of a new society.

In Marx, on the other hand, all these shortcomings seem to be eliminated. The system's laws are investigated and discovered

1 F. Engels, *Anti-Duehring* (Moscow, 1962), p. 121.
2 Ibid., pp. 365–6.
3 V. I. Lenin, *Collected Works* (Moscow, 1960), vol. XIX, p. 27.

in their objective consistency as if they were processes of natural history. Moral indignation, invective and condemnation, in so far as they remain, are framed and imprisoned in the network of scientific discourse and its rigorous demonstrations.

Marx writes in the Preface to *Capital*:[1]

> And even when a society has got upon the right track for the discovery of the natural laws of its movement – and it is the ultimate aim of this work to lay bare the economic law of motion of modern society – it can neither clear by bold leaps, nor remove by legal enactments, the obstacles offered by the successive phases of its normal development. . . . My standpoint, from which the economic formation of society is viewed as a process of natural history, can less than any other make the individual responsible for relations whose creature he socially remains, however much he may subjectively raise himself above them.

The most obvious sign of the transformation which the subject-matter of utopian socialism undergoes in Marx is the way *Capital* treats the problem of exploitation. This theme, traditionally an object of 'moral' consideration, becomes the argument of the theory of surplus value. There is no longer any appeal, as in Proudhon, to the idea of *justice éternelle*. Exploitation is no longer denounced as a theft, an 'injustice', or a violation of legality. Rather, *Capital* attempts to demonstrate how the production of surplus value is perfectly compatible with the law of exchange of commodities based on equivalence. As Marx put it:[2]

> The circumstance, that on the one hand the daily sustenance of labor-power costs only half a day's labor, while on the other hand the very same labor-power can work during a whole day, and that consequently the value which its use during one day creates is double what he pays for that use, this circumstance is without doubt a piece of good luck for the buyer, but by no means an injury to the seller.

The same notion is reiterated some years later in the so-called *Randglossen zu Wagner*. After denying that the profit made by the capitalist can be called a theft from the worker, Marx writes:[3]

1 K. Marx, *Capital* (Moscow, n.d.), vol. I, p. 10.
2 Ibid., p. 194.
3 K. Marx, 'Randglossen zur Adolph Wagners *Lehrbuch der politischen Oekonomie*', in Marx-Engels, *Werke*, (Berlin, 1955), vol. XIX.

I depict the capitalist as a necessary functionary of capitalist production and show that he does not only deduct what he is said to 'steal', but forces the *production of surplus-value* and therefore helps to create what is subsequently deducted. In addition, I simply show that in the very exchange of commodities *only equivalents* are exchanged, and that the capitalist – as soon as he has paid the worker the actual value of his labor-power – expropriates the *surplus-value* with full right, i.e., with the right corresponding to this mode of production.

For Marx, this is the explanation of the genesis of surplus value, which in the old socialism was the object of moral considerations concerning 'justice' and 'equality.' Throughout his work, Marx follows it in its activity as the propelling element of capitalist accumulation. And from surplus value, always seen as the antithesis of wage labor, he derives other categories such as profit, rent and interest, in a way which reconstructs in broad outline the entire social mechanism.

Thus, Marx frees himself from utopian socialism by becoming an economist and a scientist, by carrying on the investigation where Smith and Ricardo left off. The antithesis of bourgeois society is no longer depicted as a subjective ideal *external* to it. Instead, it is discovered within this very society: it is the contradiction between capital and wage labor. Since from the strictly economic viewpoint wage labor itself is part of capital, i.e. variable capital, the contradiction between the two ultimately results in a contradiction embodied in capital itself, an *internal* contradiction in the mechanism of capitalist accumulation.

So far we have dealt only with Marx's attitude towards utopian socialism. Concerning his attitude towards classical political economy, the argument must in a sense be reversed. Whereas Marx answers the utopian as an *economist*, he answers Smith and Ricardo as a *critic of political economy*. In both cases his critique hinges on history. However, there is a difference which must be pointed out. Marx brings against the utopians an historical understanding of real processes, an actual comprehension of existing conditions, and therefore of the mechanism of accumulation. On the other hand, history is brought against the economists in that its relativism disposes us to recognize types of society other than the existing one, both those existing in the past and those *possible in the future*. History can prevent economists from 'becoming immersed in bourgeois production as production in itself.'

Thus in the first case Marx points out that Sismondi 'convincingly criticizes the contradictions of bourgeois production without *understanding* them, thus also failing to understand the process of their dissolution.'[1] In the second case he observes that 'bourgeois economists consider capital as an external and *natural* (not historical) form of production.' That is, 'bourgeois limitations consider capitalist forms of production as absolute forms, i.e., as the eternal natural form of production.'[2]

In other words, while the disagreement with the utopian socialists has to do with the inability of their analysis to comprehend the mechanisms of capitalist production from within, the crux of the critique of political economy is the opposite. It is that Smith and Ricardo failed to see the historical relativity of the capitalist system and, mistaking it for the absolute form of production, remained its prisoners, unable to stand outside it, to grasp it as a whole and to criticize it in its totality. This critique is quite evident in the analysis of commodities at the beginning of *Capital* and permeates the theory of value. In fact, in considering the production of commodities as the universal and inevitable form of production in every possible society, Smith and Ricardo end up regarding the 'commodity-form' taken by all the products of labor under capitalist conditions as a constant, a datum of their investigation, a non-problematic fact. Marx writes: 'If Ricardo believes that the *commodity*-form is neutral, this follows from his hypothesis that the bourgeois mode of production is absolute and therefore a mode of production without more precise specific determinations.'[3]

It follows, first of all, since Smith and Ricardo assume that the product of labor always assumes the commodity form, that economics as a science simply reduces to the 'science of commodity-production.' Unable to imagine other modes of production, political economy makes the particular historical mode of production into what the motion of bodies is for mechanics, a datum which cannot be gone beyond and which cannot be left out of consideration. Second, since political economy regards commodity-production as the universal and inevitable form of social production, economic problems assume a purely quantitative character, and political economy never poses the problem of why the product of human labor in determinate historical conditions

1 K. Marx, *Storia delle teorie economiche* (Turin, 1958), vol. III, p. 59.
2 K. Marx, *Grundrisse der Politischen Oekonomie* (Berlin, 1953), p. 364.
3 K. Marx, *Storia delle teorie economiche*, vol. II, p. 582.

takes on the 'commodity-form' and why human social labor therefore appears as the 'value of things.' Instead, having assumed commodities as the irreducible datum, it restricts itself to investigating the basic quantitative relations whereby commodities are exchanged among themselves. That is, it investigates 'exchange value' rather than value proper and the social relations hidden in it.

With Marx all of these problems undergo a profound transformation. Commodity-production, far from being the universal and inevitable form of economic life, becomes only one of its possible forms. Obviously, this form has been customary for centuries and still dominates the modern era. Yet it is none the less an historically conditioned form which cannot in any way claim to be a direct manifestation of 'human' nature. Also due to Marx, as Sweezy points out, is the fact that the economist can no longer 'limit his attention to the quantitative relations arising from the production of commodities,' but 'must also pay attention to the character of the social relations underlying the form of "commodities"'; 'in the case of exchange value there is, as Adam Smith saw, the quantitative relation between products; hidden beyond this, as Marx was the first to see, there is a specific, historically conditioned, relation between producers.'[1]

This broadening of the domain of political economy, which follows from the need to go beyond that commodity-production which is the fundamental element for Smith and Ricardo, corresponds in Marx to the fact that his theory of value is *also* a *theory of fetishism* of commodities and of capital. It is a theory through which he not only limits the confines of the whole system from the outside but also uncovers the character of the inverted reality in which human relations appear as relations among things and things appear to have social qualities.

In other words, the scientific perspective, pushed to its extreme consequences, becomes for Marx a revolutionary project. The need for the *socialist* transformation reappears from within the economic analysis. Thus, it is not sufficient to understand and *explain* the production of commodities: it must be *abolished*. The material and social conditions within which the fetishistic inversion takes place must be reversed. Even when explained and understood, the mechanism whereby human social labor appears in the objective form of ownership of things and the world of products dominates the producer does not thereby cease to exist and

1 P. M. Sweezy, *The Theory of Capitalist Development* (New York and London, 1968), p. 25.

function. 'The recent scientific discovery, that the products of labor, so far as they are values, are but material expressions of the human labor spent in their production, marks, indeed, an epoch in the history of the development of the human race.' But, Marx continues, it 'by no means dissipates the mist through which the social character of labor appears to us.'[1]

Thus, science is not enough, since it is not just a matter of correcting Smith's and Ricardo's interpretation of reality but of correcting reality. The mystification is continually generated by the objective processes of capitalist production, even before it reaches the economists' level of reflection. The basic inversion, according to which wage labor – the source of capital – becomes dependent on it, while capital – only its product – comes to dominate the producer, is not due to Smith and Ricardo. It is within the very mechanism of capitalism, in which 'it is not the worker that uses the working conditions, but, on the contrary, the working conditions that use the worker.'[2]

In a nutshell, science is not enough if 'in this mode of production everything is represented upside-down.' The very social process must be inverted. In fact, political economy is not a true science. Only the revolution is the true science. Since labor must dispose of capital instead of the reverse, the only treatise that can enunciate this scientific axiom is the socialization of the means of production.

In this total *negation* of the capitalist system, all the themes enunciated by utopian socialism reappear in an even more pronounced and audacious form. The socialization of the means of production means this: the abolition of commodity production and therefore the abolition of money as well; the abolition of the market or buyer-seller relations and therefore of all the contractual and juridical forms that have come about with exchange; the abolition of the state and therefore, the transformation of politics into the 'administration of things.' All 'utopianism' reappears from within science itself.

The true remaining difference from utopian socialism is the nature of the *negation* of the system. It is no longer merely an ideal or an external subjective criterion but a real factor inherent in capitalism itself. In this case, the negation is wage-labor or the working class. It produces its own means of subsistence and, at the same time, surplus-value: profit, rent and interest. By its labor, it supplies the revenues of all fundamental classes of society. In fact,

1 Marx, *Capital*, p. 74.
2 K. Marx, *Il Capitale* (Rome, 1951), vol. I, book II, p. 129.

as long as it is subordinated to capital, the working class is only a gear in the capitalist mechanism. It appears only as 'variable capital', as part of that capital which is actually its own product. This is the inverted or upside-down society mentioned earlier. However, reinforced as it is by capitalist development, the working class organizes itself, and its consciousness matures in opposition to the whole system. It becomes the lever that can overthrow the whole system. It becomes the lever that can overthrow the whole society: the *negation* that can become real.

To summarize: all of Marx's work appears as both a revolutionary project and a scientific analysis. It is the theoretical reconstruction of the system's functioning and development while at the same time it is the consciousness of the fact that under this mode of production everything appears 'upside-down.' In the first case, Marx the *economist* continues Smith's and Ricardo's work. In the second, Marx is the *critic of political economy*, precisely in the sense that political economy is *bourgeois* political economy.

Two different interpretations of the theory of value, which must now be indicated, correspond to these two different perpectives. The first is the interpretation whereby the theory of value appears to be a 'regulative principle' which allows the explanation of the system's internal functioning. Hilferding:[1]

> if we consider the complexity of proportional relations which are indispensable in a system of production, no matter how anarchic it may be, we immediately face the problem of who cares to uphold these relations. Clearly, only the law of prices and their variations determine the expansion or the limitation of production, the starting of new production, etc. Here, too, we find the indispensability of an objective law of value as the only possible regulative element of capitalist economics.

Sweezy also considers this interpretation. After noticing that 'the law of value is essentially a theory of general equilibrium', he points out that 'this implies that one of the primary functions of the law of value is to make clear that in a commodity-producing society, in spite of the absence of centralized and coordinated decision-making, there is order and not simply chaos.' He goes on:[2]

> No one decides how productive effort is to be allocated or how much of the various kinds of commodities are to be produced,

1 R. Hilferding, *Il Capitale finanziario* (Milan, 1961), p. 335.
2 Sweezy, op. cit., p. 53.

yet the problem does get solved, and not in a purely arbitrary and unintelligible manner. It is the function of the law of value to explain how this happens and what the outcome is.

Along this same line, and with the advantage of being able to indicate its birthplace in Smith and Ricardo, he also adheres to Dobb's interpretation of the law of value.[1]

Only with the work of Adam Smith, and its more rigorous systematization by Ricardo, did political economy create that unifying quantitative principle which enabled it to make postulates in terms of the general equilibrium of the economic system – to make deterministic statements about the general relationships which held between the major elements of the system. In political economy this unifying principle, or system of general statements cast in quantitative form, consisted of a theory of value.

As can readily be seen here, the theory of value is the 'live-wire' that allows us to understand how everything which appears at first sight irrational and fortuitous in the system is actually regulated and dominated by an internal rationality. From value to prices of production and even up to market prices, from surplus-value to profit and up to equalization of profits through competition, the entire capitalist system, which appears at first sight to be totally chaotic, turns out to be a fundamentally balanced organism in which every party is in harmonious correspondence with the others. From this viewpoint, political economy appears to Marx himself as a science whose structure is not at all different from that of all other sciences. In the same way as physics studies falling bodies, economics as a science analyzes and describes the 'natural laws' of capitalist production, the same laws discussed in the Preface to *Capital*. These laws are objective material processes, 'actual operating *tendencies* functioning according to their own iron law.'

Moreover, like the natural sciences, political economy also turns out to be in a *positive* relation to its object. Here, in fact, the object, i.e. 'the development of the economic formation of society' understood 'as a process of natural history,' is not qualified as an upside-down reality to be 'negated.' (From the scientific viewpoint, these qualifications are meaningless since science's task is to explain 'facts' or 'sure phenomena' and nothing else). Rather, it is

1 Maurice Dobb, *Political Economy and Capitalism* (New York, 1945), p. 5.

treated as a self-sufficient reality whose functioning must be understood. This aspect of the theory of value is clearly indicated in the expressions of the authors just quoted. The law is a law of 'general equilibrium.' It explains how, notwithstanding all friction and contradictions, the system functions, and how a new order regularly appears out of chaos.

In the other interpretation, the law of value is the theory of *fetishism*. In this case, too, it is claimed that 'the production of commodities ... has its peculiar, inherent laws' which obtain 'despite anarchy' and which 'affect the individual producers.'[1] But in this case, the 'natural' and 'objective' character of these laws is only the *fetishistic* projection of the social relations under certain conditions: when, instead of being dominated by men, they have escaped human control. In this sense, the laws of the market obtain for men with a 'natural necessity' and the movements of the market are as unpredictable as earthquakes, not because the market is a 'natural' phenomenon, but because what has taken the objective form of *things* and of *processes among things* are the social relations among men themselves.

The difference is evident. In the first case the law of value is a theory of 'general equilibrium' which *explains* the functioning of the system; in the second it is a theory which enunciates the reasons why men must *overthrow* the system (eliminate commodity production and proceed to full socialization) if they want to free themselves from the determinism of the market and dominate their own relations. It is in this context that Engels correctly talks about a 'leap of humanity from the reign of necessity to the reign of freedom.' Furthermore, this second interpretation of the law of value not only expresses the fundamental contradiction through which labor, the source of capital, becomes its product; it also clearly implies that the only force which can overthrow the system is not a mechanical factor but the proletariat's ability to transform itself from a subordinate internal element of capitalism into a *subjective, political* external agent antithetical to the whole system.

In the opposing pull of these two different perspectives, all of Marx's work may seem to break apart and hence to give rise to antinomies.

But before surrendering to philosophical scepticism, it is worthwhile thinking again. It is true that the law of value is both the principle that regulates the *equilibrium* of the system and the principle that expresses its fundamental *contradiction*. It is true

1 F. Engels, *Anti-Duehring*, p. 372.

that the law of value is both the principle that *explains the existence* of the system and that of its *negation*. But the point is that although capitalism is a mode of production mined with radical contradictions, it remains an existing, functioning system and one's theory may deal with it simultaneously in two ways. It must be able to demonstrate both how lack of harmony and radical contradiction constantly interact in an 'equilibrium' marked by 'proportion' and 'measure' (for otherwise, the system would not exist) and also how this order constantly breaks down into disordered movement.

Marx is very clear on this point even at the very beginning of his investigations.

> The economists say that the *average price* of commodities is equal to the cost of production; that this is a *law*. The anarchical movement, in which rise is compensated by fall and fall by rise, is regarded by them as chance. With just as much right one could regard the fluctuations as the law and the determinations by the costs of production as chance, as has actually been done by other economists.

Marx concludes: 'The total movement of this disorder is its order. In the course of this industrial anarchy, in this movement in a circle, competition compensates, so to speak, for one excess by means of another.'[1]

This is not empty sophism, as it may appear at first sight. In fact, if Marx's work were not both a *critique* of capitalism, an analysis of the *internal* contradictions undermining it, and at the same time an exposition and reconstruction of the way in which, despite everything, the contradictions are overcome and the system *exists and functions*, it would amount to the empty simplicity of one of the following two errors. It would 'demonstrate too much:' overemphasize the internal contradictions of the system and thus demonstrate not just the contradictory nature of the existing system but also the *impossibility* of its existence and functioning (e.g. Sismondi or even Rosa Luxemburg). Or, it would be forced to repeat the opposite error of those who are caught and impressed by the *existence* of the mechanism under investigation, play down its internal disequilibrium to the point of rendering its existence *absolute and eternal*, and therefore fail to see why the system cannot function and last forever (e.g. Tugan-Baranowski and, in a certain sense, even Kilferding and Otto Bauer).

1 K. Marx, 'Wage, Labour and Capital', *Selected Works*, vol. I, p. 87.

Similarly, it seems that even the antinomy discussed earlier can somehow be resolved. I mean the antinomy whereby Marx's work is seen sometimes as the discovery and the *noticing* of objective material processes, and at other times as the unmasking of that false *fetishistic* 'objectivity' into which human social relations are transformed when they escape social control. Although it is impossible to analyze this fully here, the solution can probably be found by reconsidering the unity of economic-material-objective factors and socio-historical or subjective factors, upon which the unity of economics and sociology is built in Marx. In fact, as Schumpeter put it:[1]

> in the Marxian argument sociology and economics pervade each other. In intent, and to some degree also in actual practice, they are one. All the major concepts and propositions are hence both economic and sociological and carry the same meaning on both planes – if, from our standpoint, we may still speak of two planes of argument. Thus, the economic *category*, 'labor,' and the social *class*, 'proletariat,' are in principle at least made congruent, in fact, identical. Or the economists' functional distribution – that is to say, the explanation of the way in which incomes emerge as returns to productive services irrespective of what social class any recipient of such a return may belong to – enters the Marxian system only in the form of distribution between social classes and thus acquires a different connotation.

Yet, after having evaluated everything, one problem remains. Let us face it squarely. A *theory of economic collapse* aims at demonstrating scientifically, from well-established propositions, the necessity of collapse. Is there, or is there not, a theory of collapse in Marx? If we examine the debate on this point between Marx's followers and interpreters, we notice that all divergences eventually boil down to this. For some, denying that Marx's work contains a theory of collapse amounts to betraying his thought, emasculating it, and depriving it of meaning. For others, it is a betrayal to attribute one to him, even in good faith.

In the uncertainty of these alternatives, it would be very useful, at least in terms of a preliminary orientation, if it were possible to associate either of these positions with a political tendency. But another complication surrounds the theory of collapse: it is thought to exist in Marx by interpreters on the 'Right' and also

1 J. A. Schumpeter, *Capitalism, Socialism and Democracy* (New York and Evanston, 1962), p. 45.

on the 'Left.' Both the father of 'revisionism,' Bernstein, and his most ferocious and intransigent adversary, Rosa Luxemburg, attributed such a theory to Marx. On the other hand, Kautsky and Lenin, along with the social democrat, Hilferding, and the Left-wing Bolshevik, Bukharin, claimed the opposite.

My own opinion is that there is a theory of collapse in Marx's work but that it also contains reasons which lead one to deny, in principle, the validity of any such theory. Let us leave aside the question of the periodic recurrence of crises and their progressive worsening, which is elaborated less conclusively in Marx's work.

'The law of the tendential fall of the rate of profit' is a real theory of collapse. The term 'tendential' should not mislead us. In fact, it indicates that the law as such is restrained by the action of antagonistic causes which 'counteract and neutralize the action of the general law, thus giving it the character of a simple tendency'. This does not mean that the law is annihilated or overcome but rather that its 'complete realization is obstructed and slowed down.' The law operates, but over a longer time span and through a more complicated process. If this were not so, it would be difficult to understand how we can speak of it as a *law*.

Because of its very structure, this law allows us to understand what Marx means when in the Preface to *Capital* he talks about 'laws of nature, i.e. of objective material processes of the capitalist mode of production.' The law outlines a process in which the increase of the 'organic composition' of capital cannot in the long-run be compensated for by the increase in the rate of exploitation or the rate of surplus-value. Hence, it ends up expressing a relation whereby 'constant capital' and 'variable capital' are internal to capital itself rather than social classes, and the law's realization is a mechanical development.

The mechanism is as follows. To increase surplus-value and therefore profit, the capitalist must increase the productivity of labor. He must introduce technological innovations. But the introduction of these new techniques (better machinery, etc.) increases the 'organic composition' of capital, the percentage of constant capital with respect to all the invested capital. In other words, it increases a factor which decreases the rate of profit more than it can be increased by raising the rate of exploitation. The process is like that of a motor which runs into trouble because of the very mechanisms that make it function. It is not influenced in any way by the class-struggle or by the consciousness of the participants.

As a consequence, Maurice Dobb feels the need in interpreting the law to subject it to such severe limitations that its very consistency is threatened. He writes:[1]

> This law of motion could not be given a purely technological interpretation, could not be made a simple corollary of a generalization concerning the nature of changes in productive technique. The actual outcome of this interaction of conflicting elements might be different in one concrete situation from what it was in another and different situation. There is often a tendency . . . to give Marx's view of this matter a too mechanistic twist, depicting it as though it relied on the forecast of profit falling in a continuous downward curve until it reached a point at which the system would come to an abrupt stop, like an engine with insufficient pressure of steam behind the piston. The true interpretation would seem to be that Marx saw tendency and counter-tendency as elements of conflict out of which the general movement of the system emerged.

Dobb's concern is legitimate. Unfortunately, he ends up defending the law in the very same way that critics reject it. Tendency and counter-tendency balance each other; the result of this interaction varies with different situations; there is no way of predicting which of the two tendencies will eventually prevail. These are the same arguments adduced by Sweezy to attack the law. 'If both the organic composition of capital and the rate of surplus-value are assumed variable, as we think they should be, then the direction in which the rate of profit will change becomes indeterminate.'[2] More specifically: 'whether their [the capitalists'] actions will succeed in restoring the rate of profit, or whether they will only act to hasten its fall, is an issue which cannot be settled on general theoretical grounds.'[3] Certainly, the 'subjective' elements reassert themselves here; but the validity of the law is completely destroyed. The system is not destined to an inevitable collapse through a mechanical impasse. The only factor that *can* destroy it is the clash of classes, a clash in which there are, besides objective material conditions, all the necessary subjective factors, such as 'class-consciousness,' the degree of class unity and organization, and the efficacy of each class's 'political instrument.'

It can be objected that this last formulation is closest to the spirit of Marx's doctrine. In fact, Marx was never a determinist.

1 Dobb, op. cit., pp. 109–10.
2 Sweezy, op. cit., p. 102.   3 Ibid., pp. 105–6.

The statement which best summarizes all his thought is that it is men who make history, even though they do it in conditions not of their choice. But to the extent that the subject of *Capital* is capital itself and not the human wage-labor that produces it (which appears as a simple moment in the self-evaluation of capital, i.e. as 'live' labor *incorporated* in its 'dead' objectivity), it is understandable that the end of capitalism can at times be seen precisely in terms of a 'sharp stop' in the functioning of the motor of accumulation.

Let us put aside many hypotheses that come to mind: those having to do with the 'young' and the 'old' Marx and also Korsch's arguments in *Marxism and Philosophy* about the different historical natures of the two periods with which Marx dealt (the first dominated by the revolutionary climate of 1848 and the second by the stabilization of capital and the absence of working-class initiative). Let us also leave aside the question raised by Carr in *1917* about the possibility of defining Leninism as a 'return to the young Marx.'

What is to be stressed is how the consciousness of what has been said occasionally seems to flash through Marx's own pages. In chapter 15, volume III of *Capital*, precisely in the section dealing with the 'tendential fall of the rate of profit,' Marx writes:[1]

What worries Ricardo is the fact that the rate of profit, the stimulating principle of capitalist production, the fundamental premise and driving force of accumulation, should be endangered by the development of production itself. And here the quantitative proportion means everything. There is, indeed, something deeper behind it, of which he is only vaguely aware. It comes to the surface here in a purely economic way – i.e. from the bourgeois point of view, within the limitations of capitalist understanding, from the standpoint of capitalist production itself – that it has its barrier, that it is relative, that it is not an absolute, but only a historical mode of production corresponding to a definite limited epoch in the development of the material requirements of production.

If my interpretation is correct, the falling rate of profit and the *quantitative* relation it expresses are offered as the characterization of the historical and therefore transitory character of capitalism. Yet that characterization is a matter of the 'bourgeois point of view,' the viewpoint which remains 'within the limitations of

1 *Das Kapital* (Berlin, 1951), vol. III, p. 288.

capitalist understanding,' the viewpoint of capitalist production itself. However, the failure of capitalism should not be seen by socialists as a theory of collapse, that is, in 'purely economic' terms.

In other words, objective tendencies such as the falling rate of profit make sense only to the extent that they appear as conditions and real premises of the class-struggle, i.e. of the clash at a political and subjective level. Alone they have no decisive value. The illusion that they have such value generates the various theories of collapse. However, if although the true conditions of capitalism are always class-contradictions, the outcome of the clash cannot be predicted in advance. It can be objected that subjective factors are always themselves moments of reality. But then the problem becomes the following: either the subjective datum is itself as calculable as an objective datum, in which case we are back in the theory of collapse, or it is not, in which case social science can never come up with a prediction of the outcome of the process. In the latter case, the problem remains as to whether social science can still be called a science.

This is the problem with Sweezy's argument in opposing the law of the falling rate of profit, when he assumes that 'both the organic composition of capital and the rate of surplus-value are assumed variables' and concludes that 'the direction in which the rate of profit will change becomes indeterminate.' Here, the course of the historical process turns out to be not predetermined. The proposition asserting the possible equivalence between the increase in organic composition and the increase in the rate of surplus-value seems more like a simple restatement of the problem than its solution.

Here, the opposition between Bernstein and Luxemburg seems to contain something typical. If the end of capitalism cannot be scientifically demonstrated, then the foundation of the socialist program falls back on subjective ideals. It becomes an idealistic foundation and there is no longer any objective necessity, a foundation based on the material-social process. On the other hand, if that end is scientifically demonstrated as the unavoidable outcome of objective law, then we somehow end up in the theory of collapse. The subjective intervention, the consciousness of the participants, while it 'can shorten and lessen the birth-pangs' of the new society, can, 'neither clear by bold leaps, nor remove by legal enactments, the obstacles offered by the successive phases of its normal development.'

7 Alienation as a Social and Philosophical Problem

ADAM SCHAFF

1 Alienation and its definition

Let us begin not with theoretical formulations, but with a description of definite social facts. This will enable us to advance to theoretical generalizations.

Various people (groups of different sizes and sometimes single individuals) produce various objects which serve to satisfy various human needs: tables, chairs, clothes, food, houses, TV sets, automobiles, and so on. They thus produce objects for use (use values), which, however, reach the possible consumers not directly, but through market systems of various kinds. We say that they produce for the market (i.e. for anonymous consumers), and hence that objects for use appear as commodities. An object for use which appears on the market as a commodity begins to live its own specific life, governed by the market laws of demand and supply. Under certain conditions this results in perturbations which may cause social repercussions on a wide scale: depressions, unemployment in those branches of production which are affected by depression, etc., etc. Material products of human labour, intended to satisfy given human needs, function as market commodities in a way which is independent of the intentions of their producers, and in some cases they are even handled by the market in a way which is in contradiction with those intentions and which endangers the interests of the producers or simply destroys them economically.

Consider these different facts. Scientists for at least two generations have striven to make use of nuclear energy. Today we know in detail the fascinating history of their efforts, which came to be organically connected with the history and the outcome of the Second World War. Man has succeeded in an exploit which undoubtedly is a milestone on his road to understanding the secrets of the universe. When the large numbers of scientists throughout the world set themselves the given research task they certainly had in view, above all, a better comprehension of the structure of matter and the conquest of new and practically unlimited sources of energy. Only later, during the Second World War, the group of scientists headed by Fermi and sponsored by Einstein succeeded in solving the problem in practice. They had military goals in view, the warding off of the threat of the Nazi *Wunder-waffe*. What is the result of those endeavours of two generations of scientists throughout the world? The secret of nuclear energy has been unveiled and mankind has thereby acquired unprecedented and unknown sources of energy. This has opened new vistas in the development of mankind, whose power can now vie with that of ancient gods. But at the same time mankind has come to face the danger of annihilation: the threat of a total destruction has become real. This is not because anyone wants it; no one, except a mad-man, wants to perish as a result of a total war. However, mankind has proved helpless when confronted with its invention.

This is a classical example of the fact that human products can, under certain circumstances, start living their own life, inde-pendently of and even against the intentions of their makers. This is a case of the sorcerer's disciple, who knows the magical formula needed to set a certain force in operation but does not know the formula which would enable him to master that force and use it in accordance with his will.

Let us now consider another sphere of social life, social in-stitutions. These have not been parachuted from the skies either, but are human products, specific products of human thought and human labour. Obviously, in this case, the history of mankind is involved. We have to do with social products to be viewed in a historical perspective, but this merely complicates the situation, and does not alter the characteristic traits with which we are concerned. We may take into account the complication in dis-cussing, for example, that special social institution which is the state. We are interested, above all, in two functions of that in-stitution which, following Engels, we shall term 'the management of people' and 'the management of things'. By the former we shall mean the repressive function of the state, the function of en-forcing obedience by means of physical power, institutionalized within the state in the police, the courts and the army. By the latter we shall mean the administrative function, institutionalized within the state as the bureaucratic machinery.

In both its forms, as is shown by the history of state institutions, including their recent history, the apparatus of the state, while being a human product, rises above man and often against man.

Further, according to the conditions prevailing in a given period and a given social formation, the apparatus begins to function independently of the intentions of its makers and sometimes becomes their formidable and even terrible opponent. Examples are provided by the history of various police forces (especially forces of secret police) active in the various social formations. The most horrifying examples are provided by the history of wars, in which the military machine of the state becomes an independent force. In everyday life we observe the estrangement of the administrative apparatus in the form of bureaucracy, a process which is not so terrifying, but which may prove even more annoying since it is connected with every part of public life.

Finally, let us consider the sphere of ideas. Various systems of ideas, including those which we call ideologies because of their links with the activities of those who strive for specified forms of social development, are human products, products of human labour, since mental work is of course a form of labour. What happens to these products of human thought? The history of the various inquisitions, not only religious in nature and not only in post-revolutionary periods (such as the period of the French Revolution), shows tellingly how systems of ideas, formulated to serve specified purposes – usually to propagate the lofty ideals of humanity and fraternity – gradually become independent and institutionalized and under certain conditions begin to function contrary to the intentions of their founders, often destroying founders and successors. Many a time in human history ideologies, given over to the love of one's neighbour, have become instruments of hatred and persecution of man by man. Many ideologies which advocated social equality have turned into instruments used in the construction of mechanisms of social inequality. Again, against the intentions of their founders.

Let us now try to generalize from these selected examples. Let us try to extrapolate that which is common to all of them despite the variety of the issues and social factors involved. At least the following common elements can be found in the cases above and in many others as well.

(a) In each case we have social activities of human beings who intentionally strive for the attainment of certain economic, political, scientific, ideological or other goals.

(b) In each case that intentional human activity, based on mental work (often in the form of scientific theories) finds its culmination in specified products of human labour: material objects intended to serve human needs; public institutions which organize social life; inventions and scientific theories; ideological systems, etc. These products of human activity are objectivizations of human thoughts and actions in the sense that both as material and spiritual goods – in the latter case we have scientific theories, ideological systems, and the like – they reach beyond the subjective sphere of human life, the sphere of human thought, and acquire objective existence. They exist outside any human mind and regardless of whether anyone thinks about them or studies them at a given moment. They thus exist independently of any cognizing mind.

(c) In each case, these products of human social activity, which have acquired objective existence, form elements of a given, historically-shaped social system and are subject to the laws of its functioning. These laws determine the place and the function of the given products of human activity, regardless of what their makers thought about them and intended them to be, regardless of their makers' wishes and intentions.

(d) As a result, in each of the above-mentioned cases (and more generally in each analogous case of social activity of human beings) such products of human activity, having acquired objective existence, can function independently of the wishes and intentions of their makers (becoming autonomous in this sense), and also against their wishes and intentions. The products can function in a manner which contradicts the wishes and intentions of their makers, endangers their interests, or indeed destroys the makers themselves.

All those social phenomena which reveal the characteristics described above are cases or manifestations of *alienation*. We have thus arrived at a definition of the process in which we are interested, not by formulating any stipulation definition, but by drawing out those characteristics which are common to a certain class of social facts and generalizing them adequately. Obviously, the adoption of this procedure has been made easier by the fact that we do possess an appropriate theory. However, someone not in possession of such a theory could arrive at the conclusion. It is obvious that terminological issues, especially when it comes to the term *alienation*, are of a secondary importance. There could obviously be no objections to replacing the term *alienation* as the name of the class of facts with which we are here concerned by some other term, provided that it conveys the essential characteristics of that relation which underlies the facts discussed above.

When we refer to alienation, the very term brings out the fact, so important to the relation, that products of man's social activity can under certain circumstances function otherwise than intended by the man or the men who made them, and that they are 'estranged' in that sense. Hence a definition of alienation. Alienation is a relation between a human agent and the product of his activity in which that product, having acquired a socially objective existence and being situated in a given social system, functions not only autonomously (independently of the intentions of the maker), but under specified conditions even against the wishes and intentions of his maker, and may endanger his interests or his very existence.

The same social facts can be interpreted from another viewpoint, these two interpretations not being mutually exclusive but complementary. I have in mind the problem of intentionality and spontaneity in social development. While human actions are always intentional, their results, and hence the processes unleashed by such actions, may be spontaneous, or not intended by the agent(s). The element of spontaneity is linked to the relation of alienation as mentioned above: social processes become spontaneous and follow a course not intended by the agent(s) just because, under a given social system, human products function otherwise than intended by their makers. That is, to use the previous philosophical formulation, human products become alienated. Appropriate countermeasures intended to eliminate the effects of the process described above may be interpreted both as countermeasures against alienation or against the spontaneity of social processes. However, alienation is not the same as spontaneity. They are merely organically interconnected: where there is alienation, social processes tend to become spontaneous. Alienation is the cause, spontaneity of social processes is the effect, and not vice versa.

We have so far interpreted alienation as an objective social relation between a human agent and the products of his activity. Products of human activity become alienated when they function socially as objective beings, in ways not intended by their maker. But is not the maker himself, *qua* agent, also subject to alienation, too? He is, and in two ways.

In the market economy man as manpower becomes a commodity and as such is subject to the general regularities which govern the alienation of commodities. This aspect of the issue, especially with respect to the alienation of human labour (both the process and the results of that labour), has been analysed in detail in classical Marxist literature.

Second, and of particular interest, there is that alienation of man which is auto-alienation. This, to be distinguished from the alienation of products of human activity contributes a new and subjective element to the problems of alienation. This issue is interesting because it takes our reflections to another level: away from the objective process of products of human activity. With the issue of auto-alienation we pass to the level of subjective experiences of human beings, the sphere of subjective facts, even though the causes of the process are objective in nature. The issue is also interesting because the recent revival of interest in the problems of alienation (which took place after the Second World War) is most intimately connected with the problems of auto-alienation. We here encounter subjective experiences as studied by the French existentialists. It has probably been due to the Existentialist connection, incidentally, that sociologists and others have come to the groundless and erroneous conclusion that the problems of alienation are identical with those of auto-alienation.

While we note the relative independence of these two spheres of alienation and reject the reduction of the problems of alienation to problems of subjective experiences of alienated human beings (and causes of that process), we must not belittle the importance of the problems of auto-alienation. The latter process emerges whenever we analyse present-day social life. Its issues, which were seen as fairly independent processes even in classical Marxist literature, require investigation and explanation.

Here there are not such plain examples as in the case of alienation in its objective sense. The problems are much more intricate and require, even if we have plain descriptions in view, skill of a literary kind. I shall confine myself to giving a general typology of the problems involved.

What precisely is meant by the term *auto-alienation*? The matter has to do with man's alienation (estrangement) from something, something which serves as a system of reference. Two cases may be singled out from among the many possibilities offered by this understanding.

First, and this is the issue most frequently raised in the literature of the subject (including the *belles lettres*), there is the estrangement of the individual from society, his feeling of being on the outside of society, with a resulting lack of participation or engagement in public life. We here have a conflict of interests between the individual and society, a situation frequently observed in the case of delinquents, especially juveniles. The process is even more strongly marked in such social phenomena as the hippie movement. The situation, talked of in terms of 'the lonely crowd', 'lost individuals', 'anarchism', and so on, reduces to a simple though extremely important fact, one which has large consequences for present-day societies, especially in advanced countries.

The fact is that in those countries, following industrialization and the resulting growth of large agglomerations of people, human communities have become in a sense mass communities. These are marked by (a) a weakening or even disappearance of traditional bonds that used to link the individual to his community (family, neighbourhood, vocation and so on), and (b) unprecedented dependence of the individual upon the social organization, an organization of which he is a small part. The new organizational forms (except for rare cases of certain groups, often political or religious, marked by extraordinary forms of inner solidarity) do not replace the old bonds of group solidarity and the resulting sense of closeness to other people. This results in an unnerving feeling of loneliness, certainly not an invention of 'the rotten bourgeoisie' and certainly not the exclusive 'privilege' of capitalist societies, although it has found in them its strongest manifestations.

The feeling of loneliness is merely an outer though striking manifestation of something with the same causes: a crisis of 'the sense of life', which in fact is a result of a collapse of existing systems of values, of socially accepted goals of human activity. What is important is not whether there are adequate social programmes and adequate ideologies, but whether these are accepted, assimilated, or interiorized by the human beings concerned. There are important, related issues here, which must not be underestimated merely because of the fact that they have bred extremist opinions and movements. The problem itself is of social importance, and hence has attracted the attention of men of letters and philosophers, as well as social scientists.

Second, with respect to auto-alienation, we may see it as concerned with the definition of man and of 'human nature'. We may take it as the estrangement of 'real man', such as he is under given empirical conditions, from 'human nature', interpreted universally and, so to say, suprahistorically. This approach is theoretically risky because of the possibilities of metaphysical speculation. If we adopt it, we have to make at least two assumptions. (a) There is a universal and suprahistorical 'human nature'.

This is doubtful, to say the least, if we go beyond the biological characteristics of human beings. (b) We have adequate anthropological knowledge which tells us what the 'human nature', with respect to which alienation takes place, really is. Given the need for this assumption, and the previous one, we must abandon this concept of auto-alienation if we wish to persist in the empirical approach.

There have also been other versions of the concept of auto-alienation, such as Feuerbach's religious one. It has to do with transferring onto a divine being certain human properties in their absolute form, thereby impoverishing man. These variations are of little significance when compared with the first type of auto-alienation specified above. We shall retain it alone since it alone complies with the requirements of scientific theory.

What remains at this point, since we have already defined the objective relation, is to define auto-alienation. It has to do essentially with a human individual's estrangement from society. It manifests itself in the experience and attitudes of the individual, and hence is a subjective phenomenon. While alienation and auto-alienation are connected, and interact with one another, they must not be run together.

2 *The origin of the theory of alienation*

So far we have proceeded as if the theory of alienation were a product of our investigations only. This is a convenient and proper way of presenting a theory. However, presentation is not discovery. It will have been evident that our analysis and presentation of empirical data was based on a previously accepted theory. Here as elsewhere, theory comes ahead of empirical study.

The genealogy of the theory of alienation is a long and intricate one. The present writer will enlarge only on that filiation of that theory which he himself accepts, the Marxist philosophy. It is obvious that this philosophy, too, was not born – as far as the problems of alienation are concerned – *in vacuo*. Rousseau and above all Hegel are forerunners of the Marxist theory of alienation. This fact, however, does not limit us to an historical account, as supposed by those who identify philosophy with its history. In what has been said in this essay, we have not been concerned with whether, how, and how far Marx drew on his predecessors when he was constructing his own theory of alienation. Marx's conception has been followed closely in all that has been said.

According to Marx, alienation is an objective relation which consists in the estrangement of products of human activity, as a result of which these products come to dominate their makers. The Marxian concept of alienation quite distinct from the existentialist one, is given in a number of passages. In the *Economic and Philosophical Manuscripts* of 1844, in the section on 'Alienated Labor', we find these.[1]

> the worker is related to the *product of his labor* as to an *alien* object.
>
> The *alienation* of the worker in his product means not only that his labor becomes an object, assumes an *external* existence, but that it exists independently, *outside himself*, and alien to him, and that it stands opposed to him as an autonomous power. The life which he has given to the object sets itself against him as an alien and hostile force.

In this early work, which is of extreme significance for the comprehension of the later development of his ideas, Marx still refers to the estrangement of a *worker*, even though all what he says refers to the alienation of his products. In *The German Ideology*, whose significance for Marxist theory is not denied even by those who distinguish sharply between the young Marx and Marx in his mature age, the problem is formulated quite clearly. It is true that for Marx the term *alienation*, which had also been used by the young Hegelians, who were criticized by him, has derogatory undertones, which he indicates by placing the term in quotation marks. The definition of the process does not leave the smallest doubt about his intention.

Marx starts from an analysis of the consequence of the division of labour for the spontaneous formation of society and says:[2]

> as long therefore as activity is not voluntarily, but naturally, divided, man's own deed becomes an alien power opposed to him, which enslaves him instead of being controlled by him.
>
> This crystallization of social activity, this consolidation of what we ourselves produce into an objective power above us,

---

1 Karl Marx, 'Economic and Philosophical Manuscripts', in Erich Fromm, *Marx's Concept of Man*, Frederick Ungar Publishing Co., New York, 1961, pp. 95–6.
2 Karl Marx and Friedrich Engels, *The German Ideology*, parts I and III, International Publishers, New York, 1963, pp. 22–4.

growing out of our control, thwarting our expectations, bringing to naught our calculations, is one of the chief factors in historical development up till now.

This 'estrangement' (to use a term which will be comprehensible to the philosophers), can, of course only be abolished given two *practical* premises.

While interpreting alienation as a specified relation which a *product* of human bears to man, Marx also emphasizes the distinct nature and the relative conceptual independence of auto-alienation as the alienation of man himself *qua* producer.

To return to the section of the *Manuscripts* referred to above, Marx continues his comments on alienation and says:[1]

So far we have considered the alienation of the worker only from one aspect; namely, *his relationship with the products of his labor*. However, alienation appears not only in the result, but also in the *process* of *production*, within *productive activity* itself. How could the worker stand in an alien relationship to the product of his activity if he did not alienate himself in the act of production itself?

What constitutes the alienation of labor? First, that the work is *external* to the worker, that it is not part of his nature, and that, consequently he does not fulfil himself in his work but denies himself, has a feeling of misery rather than well-being, does not develop freely his mental and physical energies but is physically exhausted and mentally debased. The worker therefore feels himself at home only during his leisure time, whereas at work he feels homeless.

We arrive at the result that man (the worker) feels himself to be freely active only in his animal functions ... while in his human functions he is reduced to an animal.

Marx not only very nearly introduces the term *auto-alienation* ('alienate himself'), but also clearly interprets the matter as concerning the subjective feelings and experience of a human being. He understands perfectly well that in the case of auto-alienation we have to do with an estrangement of a man from something. He assumes a system of reference. It is true that Marx takes 'the essence of man' ('human nature') as that system of reference. This, which we have tried to avoid, is not at all important. What is of

1 Karl Marx, op. cit., pp. 98–9.

decisive significance is that he distinguishes between auto-alienation and alienation and holds that the auto-alienation of a human being always is his alienation *from something*, and manifests itself in the sphere of subjective feelings and experience.

It is not possible here to engage in detailed Marxological studies of the problem of alienation. The above quotations from Marx's writings confirm the validity of ascribing certain propositions about alienation to Marx. What is to come will be less formal, without quotations. The procedure is justified by the nature of this paper.

Here then is a tentative reconstruction of the Marxist theory of alienation.

All productive activity, whether its results are material or mental, results in objectivization, which is to say that the products of that activity exist objectively, outside the minds of all cognizant subjects and independently of them. Objectivization is a necessary *fact* in man's individual and societal life.

A product of human activity is an objectivization in two senses: (a) in the sense of its objective existence (as explained above), and (b) in the sense of the fact that human thought, which underlies all conscious human activity, takes on an objectivized form. Yet, even though a deliberate intention with specified goals underlies all productive activity, the product does not always function in accordance with that deliberate intention and in accordance with the goals indicated by that intention. Since every individual lives and acts *in* society, a given product, whether material or mental, enters the existing network of social relations and functions in accordance with the laws of the latter, regardless of the intention of its maker. This applies to *all* products of human activity, and not only to marketable commodities. Marx, understandably given his activity and interests, was concerned mainly if not exclusively with the alienation of commodities and of the human labour that produces them. Nothing prevents us from formulating Marx's analyses in a more general manner. He himself engaged in such broader analyses.

While objectivization necessarily accompanies all human activity, it turns into alienation only under certain conditions. Alienation is a contingency, and not a necessity, of social life. This yields two practical conclusions. (a) Alienation can be overcome, and even prevented, if we change the social conditions in which objectivization turns into, or degenerates into, alienation. (b) Alienation is, from a societal point of view, a *permanent* danger, since any objectivization can degenerate into alienation under specified conditions, which vary according to the sphere of social life and the category of products of human activity. These are important conclusions for social engineering. We shall revert to them in the last section of this paper.

One aspect more deserves attention. The problem of alienation is organically connected with that of spontaneity in development, which was pointed out by Marx and is of course self-evident. If alienation consists in the fact that products of human activity function regardless of, and sometimes contrary to, the intentions of their makers, then societies may develop not in line with the deliberated intentions of human beings, but spontaneously. The close connections between alienation and spontaneity must be borne in mind when we pass to theoretical reflections on measures of social engineering intended to prevent processes detrimental to social development.

We have so far considered the two basic concepts in the Marxist theory of alienation: objectivization and alienation. There are two other concepts which are to be mentioned – in fact they call for deep analysis. They are closely connected with the theory, and are the concepts of reification and commodity fetishism.

In the case of both, the fundamental point is that under specified conditions, relations between human beings take on the external form of relations between things (commodities) and are veiled by those reified relations. The reified relations distort the real nature of the mechanism of social relations. Reifications and commodity fetishism therefore both have to do with consequence of the alienation of human labour. There is the proviso that reification is theoretically the broader concept of the two, since it applies not only to marketable commodities, as in the case of commodity fetishism, but also to all forms of human relations.

Linked with alienation as they are, neither reification nor commodity fetishism is conceptually identical with alienation. Nor can they replace the concept of alienation, as has been suggested by certain authors. This is so because alienation concerns all products of human activity, and not things alone, and because the relation between alienation, on the one hand, and reification and commodity fetishism, on the other, is not symmetrical. Alienation breeds reification and commodity fetishism, but not vice versa. Lukács, who in the original edition of *Geschichte und Klassenbewusstsein* raised reification to the rank of the highest concept, replacing alienation, took the other view subsequently.

To conclude this exposition of the Marxist theory of alienation, we shall look briefly at auto-alienation.

As indicated by a quotation above, Marx as early as the *Manuscripts* made a clear distinction between alienation and auto-alienation. In his text, auto-alienation is a derivative of alienation, since the former is in the sphere of subjective feelings. It does not follow in the least that auto-alienation, even if interpreted in the narrow sense of alienation from 'the essence of man', is to be underestimated. It is true that Marx did not refer to alienation in the sense of man's estrangement from society. He did not have necessary data at his disposal, given the stage and character of the development of social relationships at the time. Today nothing prevents us from extending our analysis. On the contrary, we are obliged to do so if we are to apply the Marxian method in a new social situation.

Auto-alienation is also a derivative of alienation in the sense of auto-alienation accepted above. In a world of alienated human products which reify human relations, in a world that escapes deliberate control by society and at the same time weakens, or even destroys, the traditional links between the individual and society, human relations face dangerous complications. The problem of auto-alienation, derivative as it is, is a real problem, one which requires adequate measures.

3 The origin of the resistance to the theory of alienation

Although the theory of alienation has become fashionable, it has met with objections and resistance.

Protests against the inevitable simplifications of the theory, its vulgarization, may be left outside our discussion. The same applied to the opposition of conservatives who oppose a theory which, by unveiling the real causes of social evils, works for a change in the present state of things. The theory of alienation as formulated above is aimed mainly at the class-based system of private property in the means of production. It is private property which is mainly blamed for alienation. Theoretical objections raised by the conservatives are self-explanatory and may be ignored here.

It is otherwise when we come to objections and protests raised by certain circles which officially profess the Marxist theory. This fact, in some cases connected with a social problem, is neither trivial nor quickly understandable. We must focus our attention on this fact, which is of considerable practical and theoretical importance.

Some people, claiming to defend 'orthodox' Marxist theory (and in some cases believing what they say), claim that the theory of alienation is alien to the Marxist theory. They argue that interest in it is 'revisionist' in nature and shows that Marxist revisionists have succumbed to existentialism and personalism, fashionable in bourgeois circles. They argue that if the theory of alienation is to be found in Marx's works, then this is a matter only of his youth, when he had not yet overcome the influence of bourgeois ideology. In his mature works, we are told, he firmly dissociated himself from that theory, and accordingly in those works we find neither the term *alienation* nor the problems to which the term refers. These opinions have nothing to do with 'orthodoxy', and are notoriously mistaken. We shall analyse their origins after looking briefly at their main points.

First, it is not true that Marxists concerned with the problems of alienation within the broader framework of the Marxist philosophy of man have drawn on the existentialists or followed 'fashion'. On the contrary, it was French existentialism, which after the Second World War popularized the problems of alienation, which drew on Marxism. This was made clear by such authors as Sartre. Historically, priority plainly goes to Marxism.

Second, the problems of alienation are not peripheral in the Marxist theory and are not due to Marx's 'immaturity'. They are fundamental to Marxist theory and are connected with the basic issue of Marxian socialism, the striving to overcome spontaneity and achieve an intentional and planned development of societal life as a necessary condition of many-sided human development. All other problems in the Marxist theory, whether economic, political, social or organizational, are by their very nature historically conditioned and transitory. *This* problem – the striving for planned societal development and the elimination of spontaneity – remains valid in every social formation. As we have seen above, the theory of alienation is intimately connected with the issue of spontaneous development of societies and is, as it were, its other aspect, its interpretation from another point of view. Spontaneous development takes place only when products of human activity function at variance with the intentions of their makers: in other words, become alienated.

Third, the supposition about 'two Marxes', between whom a strongly marked caesura can be observed (Althusser's notorious *coupure*), is simply false. That supposition is often made by those who do not approve of the mature Marx. By accepting only the works written in his early period, they can 'deliver' Marx for Marxism and communism. The supposition is also made by those who, in the name of supposed 'orthodoxy', reject Marx's early writings and try to dissociate all anthropological issues from Marxist theory.

This paper is not the place in which to prove the somewhat trivial truth that the various stages in the mental development of the great thinker form, for all the differences between them, a single whole, and that only a complex treatment of his opinions enables us to understand them fully. It is only by interpreting Marx's early opinions in the light of his later results that we can notice and understand those ideas which were important and fertile in his early period. Vice versa, when we view his later, mature works from the perspective of his early ideas, we can grasp their latent meanings, their intentions, and the rationales for his studies of certain issues. The claim that Marx in his mature period abandoned the study of alienation and related issues as ill-conceived and un-Marxist is a result of mere ignorance. It suffices to read Marx's *Grundrisse* of 1857, his first version of *Capital* and certainly a mature work (one often referred to by the propounders of the theory of the said *coupure* in Marx's mental development) to see that such a claim is simply absurd.

We may thus approach the problem of alienation from the standpoint of the Marxist theory and disregard objections having to do with 'revisionism' and 'bourgeois philosophers'. In both cases the evidence is to the contrary.

Let us now focus attention on how it has come about that a theory developed in connection with the focal issues of Marxism and linked with them from the very inception of the Marxist theory, and aimed at the capital system, has come to meet resistance on the part of the Marxists themselves and has been rejected in the name of supposed 'orthodoxy'. This is an intricate issue.

Two factors above all account for the negative attitude toward the problems of alienation. One is lack of sufficient knowledge of Marxist theory. The other is unwillingness to raise the problem of alienation under socialism.

The former is trivial. The point is that the generation of party activists who control the 'social demand' for ideological issues was trained in Marxist theory at a time when the problems of alienation were practically unknown. It must be borne in mind that the works of the classical Marxist authors in that field were published during the decade that preceded the Second World War, and hence could be an object of exhaustive studies only after 1945. We can easily understand the incredulity of those for whom Marxism used to be associated exclusively with economics, class struggle, etc., and who came to be confronted with problems of man, alienation, auto-alienation, etc., problems new to them *qua* elements of Marxist theory. The simplest solution was to assume that those problems were 'alien' to Marxist theory, that they were adopted 'from the outside'. Obviously, those people who write professionally of Marxist theory ought to know more, but in fact it is not always so. Also, we should not underestimate the importance of the 'social demand' which comes from party authorities and is conditioned by various social factors in social psychology.

At this point we come to the essential issue: unwillingness to engage in the study of problems which disturb tranquility. If one admits the study of the problems of alienation, it becomes embarrassing when it pertains to socialist conditions. Of course, one can assume that by definition the issue applies only to the capitalist market economy, and that with the abolition of the private property in the means of production the problem of alienation will vanish. Propounders of this claim (who refer to Marx's early writings) do in fact exist. Their reasoning obviously cannot survive criticism. In Marx's opinion, from his youth to the end of his days, the concept of alienation was much broader and covered such institutions as the state and such ideologies as religion.

What are we to do about those alienated entities which continue to survive under socialism? When the concept of alienation is interpreted broadly, we cannot avoid the logical consequence of the reasoning which shows that under specified conditions *any* objectivization may change into alienation. Is it then not possible, following changes in the social system under socialism, and even under communism, that new structures will intensify certain forms of alienation and even breed new ones? Let us notice the social fact of bureaucracy, whose growth is favoured by concentration of decision in the hands of state authorities. 'The management of things' by the state, whose vanishing was not postulated in the classical Marxist theory, will expand greatly in view of the new forms and needs of management. This management, in communism, could change in the direction of traditional forms of government. These examples, which could be multiplied, show that the issue of alienation under socialism is a real one. We must not stubbornly deny facts in order to keep up appearances. We must not behave like the bureaucrat described by Shchedrin, who wanted to 'undiscover America' in order to evade the problem he was faced with. Such a policy yields no results. Real issues must be treated as real. When we have found out their nature we must try to deal with them or prevent their emergence. That is the task of social engineering.

4 The value of the theory of alienation for social engineering

The value and the importance of the theory of alienation consists not in the description of the untoward effects of the functioning of human products. It consists in explaining them, and hence in showing what measures can eliminate them. The theory of alienation is significant for social engineering.

We have tried to find out under what conditions (under what socio-political structure) a given objectivization changes into alienation. We then have either to change the existing conditions (the structure of the system) or to resort to preventive measures which render the emergence of such conditions impossible. Present techniques of system-analysis and simulation by models enables us to find the regularities in question easily. The real difficulty is social resistance to those changes in the structure of the system which are necessary for the overcoming of alienation or for its prevention. This is resistance on the part of those who are privileged by the existing state of things. The problem is a well-known one, and is typical not only of the class system based on private property. Yet, theoretically at least, in a modelled society, it is possible to include an 'analyser of dangers of alienation' which will indicate ways of overcoming existing evils and, to some extent, warn of imminent new cases of alienation.

One point is to be stressed with special force. The problem always is one of overcoming a *given* case of alienation or a *given* form of alienation, and not alienation in general. Alienation 'in general' exists only in the sphere of ideas as an abstract concept, and cannot be encountered in real life. The fact that a *given* form or case of alienation has been overcome does not prevent other forms from emerging. Is it worth while striving to overcome a given form or case of alienation if new forms or cases may emerge? The benefit is analogous to treating a person who suffers from influenza, although he may later develop another disease. A successful treatment of a *given* illness is good for the patient, even though we realize that he is not immune to other ailments. A relapse is merely *possible*, and not necessary, and may be prevented by adequate measures.

The theory of alienation, by revealing to us the causes and origins of a social evil, helps us considerably both to fight that evil and to prevent it. It would be unreasonable not to avail ourselves of that possibility because we cannot eliminate the evil absolutely. And it is simply culpable to renounce that possibility because of one's own particular interest, or to place group interests above the interest of society as a whole. It must be borne in mind that personal or group interests, and not only under the capitalist system, veil facts and help people to fail to notice those things which they find inconvenient. The veil often takes on the form of a myth of 'orthodoxy'.

8 Philosophical Foundations of Economic and Political Self-management

MIHAILO MARKOVIĆ

Most economic, sociological and political writing on economic and political self-management takes certain basic theoretical assumptions about its meaning, its desirability and its feasibility for granted. These assumptions need to be examined, clarified and evaluated within the framework of a critical social philosophy. The latter differs from pure speculative philosophy in so far as it concentrates on the field of concrete historical possibilities, and differs from positive, specialized science in so far as it does not remain satisfied with a mere description of the actually given opportunities but also explores the hidden and latent *potential* of the historical situation. A critical theory of economic and political self-management, or simply self-management, therefore builds up syntheses of experience and wisdom, theory and practice, explanation of the given present forms of social reality and insight into future social change.

Such a theory explores the following three crucial problems:

1 What *is* the concept of self-management, in contrast to such related concepts as those of participation, workers' control, direct democracy, and decentralization?

2 What are the more basic philosophical principles which can justify the view that self-management is a desirable form of social organization?

3 Is the idea of self-management really feasible in modern industrial society? Is it a mere utopian dream or are there certain specifiable historical conditions under which it could be implemented and give rise to a rational and efficient social system?

1 The concept of self-management

The term 'self-management' may be used in a very indiscriminate way, covering a number of different social structures which either have not yet fully escaped old authoritarian and hierarchical relationships or else contain new, autonomous and equitable relationships in an incomplete and not fully developed form. I use the term in such a way that self-management is distinct from certain other things.

Worker's control is an important, progressive objective in a class society. Still, workers' control may contribute only to preventing undesirable decisions. It does not allow for the determining of a positive policy in enterprises and local communities.

Workers participation is also a progressive demand that has been gaining more and more ground in the international labor movement. It is nevertheless a broad, vague demand, and in various forms it could be accepted by the ruling class without really affecting the general social framework of a capitalist society. Workers might be given rights to participate only in decision-making on matters of secondary importance; they might be in a minority in a given body of management; they might be allowed only advisory or consultative functions and not the right to make decisions; finally, they might be denied access to information and left in a position merely to endorse decisions that have been prepared by others and presented without real alternatives.

The dictatorship of the proletariat, which in Marx's theory refers to a transition period of the 'withering away' of the state and of increasing democratization, is nowadays associated with the existence of a strong, centralized authoritarian state actually in the hands of a political bureaucracy. Such a state uses the phrases 'the power of Soviets' or 'workers' state' in order to conceal and mystify the real oppressive nature of social relationships.

Participatory democracy refers to a social form in which the freedom of citizens is not reduced to an occasional election of representatives who rule 'in the name of the people', but involves the right of direct participation in decision-making. This is more then the classical liberal conception of democracy, which turns out to be rule by consent of a silent majority easily manipulated. This is also more than mere 'participation' because it specifies that what is in question is not any insignificant participation but participation in government. However, participatory democracy is less than self-management, since it is not clear whether first, this form of democracy embraces the economic sphere as well as the political one, and second, whether the totality of social power stays in the hands of the people or remains in considerable part a monopoly of a center of alienated economic and political power.

The idea of self-management is not to be confused either with the idea of a mere *decentralization*. An atomized and disintegrated society, lacking coordination and conscious regulation, would be at the mercy of blind and alienated social forces. Self-management is not the absence of any management and conscious direction within the society as a whole in matters of common interest. These include economic development, communications and transportation, health service, social security, education, macro-projects of general social importance in science and culture.

Self-management cannot be reduced to *direct democracy*. If it is to be an integral form of organization of the whole society, and not only the organizational from of enterprises and local communities (which would require the existence of the classical state), self-management involves not only an immediate commitment at the level of social micro-structure but also *delegation* of social power at the level of the macro-structure. In contrast to the 'people's representatives' who constitute the apparatus of the classical democratic state, the delegates who would constitute the self-managing organs of the global society (the republic, the federation) would not be professional politicians. They would be elected, rotatable and devoid of material privileges.

The idea of self-management derives from a more general philosophical conception – that of *self-determination*.

Self-determination is a process in which conscious practical activity of human individuals becomes one of the necessary and sufficient conditions of individual and group life. This is a process contrary to *external* determination, i.e. a process in which the necessary and sufficient conditions of the life of some human individuals are exclusively factors outside their control and independent of their consciousness and will.

To be sure, self-determination is always conditioned by a given social situation, by the level of technology, the given structure of production, the nature of political institutions, the level of culture, the existing tradition and habits of human behaviour. However, it is essential for self-determination, first, that all these external objective conditions constitute only the framework of possibilities of a certain course of events, and that it depends upon subjective choice and conscious human activity which possibilities will be realized. Second, it is essential that the subjective choice is autonomous, genuinely free and not heteronomous or compulsory. This means that the subject by his own activity creates a new condition of the process, instead of merely repeating an act to which he was compelled or for which he was programmed. This act need not be arbitrary and groundless, and should be an act of self-realization, of the actualization of basic human capacities, of the satisfaction of genuine human needs.

This active role in the course of events, this creation of new conditions rather than a mechanical reproduction according to the laws of the system and inherited instincts, this extension of the framework of possibilities rather than a mere persistence within that framework – this is a specific power of men, characteristic of every human individual, present at least in the form of a latent disposition.

Under certain social conditions this power can be *alienated*. It can be concentrated in the hands of a privileged social group and become its monopoly. Alienation is a consequence of (1) a professional division of labor, (2) the accumulation of surplus-product, (3) the creation of institutions whose function is to take care of common social interests, (4) increasing mediation between individual needs and the needs of the whole society. Political and economic alienation involves a process of social polarization which on the one hand transforms a conscious and potentially creative subject into an object, a reified, oppressed and exploited mass, and on the other hand transforms a normal, limited and fragile human subject into an authority, a mystified entity regarded as having supernatural power and in fact having control over human lives.

Such a critical analysis of self-determination and alienation leads to this question: under what social conditions would the life of individuals and communities be less and less reified, less and less contingent upon external authority, and more and more self-determined? There are four such basic conditions:

The *first* is negative. Coordination and direction of social processes must no longer be in the hands of any institution which enjoys a monopoly of economic and political power (such as capital, or the state with its coercive apparatus, or a party with its bureaucracy, hierarchy of power and ideological manipulation). People themselves must decide on all matters of common interest. This is possible only if the society is organized as a federation of councils composed of non-professional, non-alienated representatives of the people. Such councils must exist at all levels of social structure: in enterprises and local communities, in regions and in whole branches of activity, and finally at the level of the society as a whole.

The *second* condition of self-determination is reliable knowledge of the society's situation, of its scarcities and limitations, of the existing trends, of the conflicts to be resolved, of the alternative possibilities of further development. Freedom is incompatible with ignorance or with a biased perception of reality. The right to make decisions without previous access to information is a mere formality: self-determination becomes a façade behind which there occurs manipulation by others, by a political bureaucracy and technocracy. Therefore genuine self-determination pre-supposes the formation of critical study groups at all levels of social decision-making, from the local community and enterprise to the federation as a whole.

The *third* condition of self-determination is the existence of powerful and democratic public opinion. The genuine general will of the people can be formed only through open communication, free expression of critical opinions, and dialogue. It is clear, then, that any monopoly over the mass media (either by business, or the church, or the state, or a party) must be dismantled. Such a monopoly enables a ruling élite to manipulate the population, to create artificial needs, to impose its ideology and to construe its selfish and particular interests as general ones. Therefore the *mass media* must be free and genuinely socialized.

The *fourth* condition of self-determination is the discovery of the true *self* of the community, the development of a consciousness of the real general needs of the people. This condition is basic and most difficult to achieve. Only with great effort and only in certain crucial situations does an individual, a nation or a class reach a full sense of self-identity. Therefore, most of what passes under the name of freedom in contemporary society is only an illusory freedom: mere opportunity of choice among two or more alterna-tives. The alternatives are imposed, choice is arbitrary, and even when it has been guided by a consistent criterion of evaluation, this criterion is not authentic, not based on a critical and enlight-ened examination of real needs and long-range interests. This condition clearly presupposes a universal humanist point of view, and implies in practical terms a creation of a new socialist culture and a humanist revolution of all education. Discovery of one's self and of one's specific individual powers and potential capacities, learning how to develop them and use them as a socialized human being caring about the needs of other individuals – these would be the primary aims of a new humanist education.

The achievement of these conditions of self-determination, the transition from reification and external determination to freedom and self-determination, is a matter of a whole epoch.

Existing approximations to self-management, seen in this broad historical perspective, are of great revolutionary importance but should be regarded as only initial steps. With general material and cultural development many other steps will be necessary and many present limitations will have to be overcome. The organs of the classical state (an instrument of class rule) will have to be replaced by organs of self-management composed of the delegates of workers' collectives and territorial communities. Planning of production and social development must be a synthesis of the decision-making in decentralized autonomous units of the social micro-structure and the democratic centers of the macro-structure. Market economy, with its production for profit, must gradually be replaced by production for genuine human needs. With further technological advance productivity of work can increase quickly while, at the same time, the present-day hunger for consumers' goods can be replaced by entirely different aspirations. The present-day concern about production and management will naturally tend to diminish. Self-determination in various other aspects of free and creative praxis will naturally gain in importance.

2   Basic philosophical principles

In the preceding analysis it was assumed that a model of society based on self-determination (the special case of which in the economic and political sphere is self-management), is superior to any authoritarian social model, even if only moderately authoritarian. This is a challenge not only to totalitarianism of the fascist, bureaucratic or technocratic varieties, whose intellectual and moral position is so weak that it must disguise itself by a pseudo-revolutionary, populist ideology. It is also a challenge to liberalism, which reduces human emancipation to political liberation only, and even in that narrow sphere reduces human freedom to a set of liberties and rights possessed by an individual citizen who is confronted with a permanently indispensable state. The state remains an external authority. As it is taken as out of the question that human individuals and various social groups should freely organize themselves and freely coordinate their efforts in order to take care of general social interests, they must consent to the rule of a privileged, powerful minority. On the other hand, labor remains the essential part of a 'healthy' human life, no matter how much the productivity of work increases. If law and order within a stable state and the maximization of material production remain the basic pillars of human society, then the alternative to self-management is a computerized consumer society in which increases of comfort and entertainment are the essential aspirations of the greatest part of humankind.

This liberal model of society has a well-known philosophical, ideological and religious background. Toil is taken to be an inescapable part of the human predicament. It is both a healthy outlet for human energy and a means of conquering nature. The coercive function of the state is taken as necessary in order to curb the evil, aggressive, selfish drives in human nature, and to provide peace and security.

What is the philosophical background of the model of socialist self-management? The following are the basic philosophical ideas, developed by Karl Marx and some of his followers.

1 Man is essentially a being of free, creative activity, of *praxis*.

2 Under the conditions of class society, human potential is wasted. Man is *alienated*.

3 Commodity production and political life controlled and dominated by the state are two essential forms of alienation (alienated labor and alienated politics).

4 Ruling classes have a vested interest in the preservation of alienation. Therefore human emancipation and full realization of the human potential can be achieved only through a revolutionary transformation of the whole economic and political structure and the introduction of self-management.

This whole analysis rests on a concept of human nature. Beneath a vast variety of manifested, observable features of human behaviour, there exists a permanent potential capacity of man to act in an imaginative and creative way, to produce new objects and forms of social life, to change not only his surroundings but to evolve himself. Man is often inert and passive, he occasionally manifests a strong irrational drive to destroy. In general, he has many conflicting latent dispositions: to be independent and free but also to escape responsibility, to belong to a social community but also to pursue selfish private goals, to live in peace and security but also to compete and be aggressive, etc. These latent dispositions are empirically testable in that they can be brought to life and observed when appropriate conditions are created. Some of them have been responsible for great achievements in human history and are worthy of being reinforced. Some of them have led to great disasters or long periods of decay and stagnation and need to be modified and overcome.

The capacity for *praxis* is the essential characteristic of men precisely because it was and is the necessary and sufficient condition of human history. In all real historical moments, moments of novelty, individuals and whole large collectives acted in a specifically human way. It is distinguished in the following respects.

1 Specifically human activity, *praxis*, involves a conscious and purposeful change of objects. This change is not a repetition; it introduces a novelty. Man rebels against any form of limitation, deriving from another world or from within himself. Novelty is essentially the overcoming of limitation.

2 *Praxis* is the objectification of all the wealth of the best human potential and capacities. It is an activity which is a goal in itself and free in the positive sense of a genuine self-realization. Therefore it is profoundly pleasurable for its own sake no matter how much effort and energy it requires.

3 While involving self-affirmation, *praxis* also mediates between one individual and another and establishes a *social relation* between them. In the process of *praxis* an individual is immediately aware that through his activity and his product he satisfies the needs of other individuals, enriches their life, and indirectly becomes a part of them. Through *praxis* an individual becomes a *social being*.

4 Finally, *praxis* is *universal*, in that by constant learning man is able to incorporate in his activity the modes of action and production of other living beings and other nations and civilizations.

These characteristics of specifically human, free and creative activity are very rarely evident under conditions of modern industrial production and modern political life. The work of the vast majority of human beings, owing to a series of historical conditions, does not have a specifically human character. It is a tremendous waste of human potential, *alienated labor*.

The necessity for an increase in productivity results in the division of labor, the partition of society into professional groups, the polarization of physical and intellectual workers, managers and employees, the crumbling and atomizing of the entire working process into individual phases, and finally operations around which the whole life of individuals or groups of workers is fixed. Then the entire structure of human work disintegrates and an acute gap between its constituent elements appears. The product no longer has its determined producer and the producer loses all connection with the object he has produced.

This is a *two-sided* externalization (*Entäusserung*). The product not only escapes from the control of its creator, but it begins to act as an independent power which treats its maker like an object, a thing to be used.[1] This phenomenon is possible because behind the object there is another man who uses it to transform the producer into a thing. The human qualities of the producer's labour force are completely irrelevant except for one. It is a special kind of commodity which can produce other commodities and which needs for its upkeep and reproduction a smaller amount of objectified work than the amount of objectified work which it creates. This two-sided externalization, which in essence is not a relation of a man to the natural object, but rather a specific relationship of a man toward other man, is alienation.[2]

Marx did not discover the idea of alienated labor. It can be found in Hegel's early works. However, Marx reopened a problem which Hegel supposed himself to have solved and closed. Marx gave it a real historical perspective within the framework of a general humanistic philosophical vision. While working on *Grundrissen der Kritik der politischen Oekonomie* and in his first draft of *Das Kapital*, Marx rarely used the term 'alienation' itself. The concept was the basis for Marx's entire critique of political economy.

Marx's critical position in *Das Kapital* can only be understood in the light of his hypothesis of true human community and true production where each man both 'affirms himself and the other man.'

The analysis of labor in *Das Kapital* is the starting point for the explanation and criticism of capitalist society, and of any other society which is based on commodity-production. The character of labor is contradictory. What Marx in his earlier works called 'alienated labor' is now described by the term 'abstract labor.' Only abstract labor creates exchange value and only it has a socially acknowledged importance. However, man's labor is here totally

1 'Die Entäusserung des Arbeiters in seinem Product hat die Bedeutung nicht nur, dass seine Arbeit zu einem Gegenstand, zu seiner äusseren Existenz wird, sondern, dass sie ausser ihm unabhängig, frei von ihm existiert, und eine selbststandige Macht ihm gegenüber wird,' K. Marx in *Marx–Engels Gesamtansgabe* (MEGA), vol. 1, 3, p. 83.
2 'Durch die wechselseitige Entäusserung oder Entfremdung des Privateigentums, ist das Privateigentum selbst in die Bestimmung des Entäusserung Privateigentums geraten,' *ibid.*, p. 538.

crippled, deprived of everything personal, free, creative, spontaneous, or human. It is reduced to being a simple supplement to machines. The only socially acknowledged characteristic of this labor is its quantity and this is judged by the market and receives its abstract objective form – money. The fetishism of commodities, the mysticism of the merchandise-world, are the concepts by which, within the sphere of economics, Marx expresses the same structure of productive relations which he earlier described in terms of 'alienated labor.' The point, as Marx says in *Das Kapital*, is that 'their [the commodity producers'], own historical movement takes the form of the movement of things under whose control they happen to be placed, instead of having control over them.'

The conclusion which Marx draws from his analyses of the production of relative surplus value is a conclusion which reproduces in condensed form all of the elements of his criticism of alienated labor in early writings. Within the capitalist system all methods for increasing social productive forces are carried out at the expense of the individual worker. All means for developing production degenerate into means for the exploitation of and rule over the producer. They make a cripple of the worker, a semi-man, reduce him to the common equipment of a machine, destroy the last remains of appeal in his work, transforming it into a real torture. They alienate from the worker the intellectual possibilities of the process of labor. They deform the conditions under which he works, subject him in the process of labor to a disgusting and pedantic despotism, transform his entire life into working hours, throw his family under the juggernaut's wheel of capital.

In his *Economic and Philosophical Manuscripts*, Marx distinguished four types of alienation of the worker.

1 Alienation from the product of labor, which becomes an independent blind power.

2 Alienation from the production itself, which becomes compulsive, routine, and loses any traits of creativity (which implies production according to the laws of beauty).

3 Alienation from the human generic being, for whom conscious, free and productive labor is characteristic.

4 Alienation from other men, because satisfaction of another's needs, supplementing another's being, cease to be the prime motive of production.

All of these aspects of alienation can be found in *Das Kapital*.

The fetish character of commodities lies precisely in the fact that 'the social characteristics of their own work seem to people to be characteristics which objectively belong to the products of labor themselves, to be properties which those things have by nature.' Hence, 'social relationships among people assume for them a phantasmagorical form of the relationships among things.'

This reification of human relations springs from specific characteristics of labor which produces commodities. Labor can take on the character of a commodity only 'when various specific cases of work are reduced to a common character which they all have as the expenditure of working capacity, as human labor in the abstract.' This abstract labor ceases to be a need and fulfilment of the human being and becomes the mere necessary means of its subsistence:[1]

> The accumulation of wealth at one end is at the same time the accumulation of poverty, hard labor, slavery, ignorance, growing bestiality, and moral decline at the other, that is, on the part of the class which brings forth its own product in the shape of capital.

The alienation of the producer from the other man stems from the simple fact that the purpose of the work is no longer the satisfaction of another's needs, but rather the possibility for transforming labor into money – the general and impersonal form of objectified labor. The drastic forms of alienation among people arise as a consequence of the competition, exploitation and despotism to which the worker is submitted. In order to increase production and at the same time to prevent a decline in the profit rate, it becomes necessary to squeeze from the worker an increasingly large amount of unpaid work.[2] Hence the necessity for the most efficient manipulation of workers and the need for an increase in the degree of the exploitation of labor.

Criticism of alienated labor, therefore, is present in both *Das Kapital* and in all earlier works. To lose sight of this criticism is to lose the possibility of understanding the deepest meaning of Marx's message. It is also to be in danger of succumbing to the dangerous illusion that historical problems have been already resolved when in fact all that has been realized are some preconditions.

Marx carefully explained in his earlier writings that *private property is not the cause but the consequence of alienated labor*,

1 K. Marx, *Das Kapital*, vol. 1, ch. 1, p. 4.
2 Ibid., vol. 1, ch. 23, p. 4.

just as gods are originally the consequence and not the cause of religious alienation. Only later does conditioning become reciprocal. In the society which Marx calls 'primitive,' the society of 'nonreflective communism,' 'man's personality is negated in every sphere.' The entire world of culture and civilization is negated, and regresses towards the unnatural simplicity of the poor and wantless individual, who has not only not surpassed private property, but has not yet even attained it.[1] In this kind of society, Marx says, 'the community is only a community of *work* and of *equality of wages* paid with communal capital by the community as universal capitalist.'[2]

That is why Marx felt that the basic question was that of the *nature of labor* rather than the question of private property. 'In speaking of private property, one believes oneself to be dealing with something external to mankind. But in speaking of labor one deals directly with mankind itself. This new formulation of the problem already contains its solution.'[3]

The solution, therefore, is to abolish the relations into which the worker falls during the process of his labor, to abolish the situation in which he becomes only one of the commodities in the reified world of commodities. The essence of exploitation lies in the fact that accumulated, objectified labor – capital – rules over live work and appropriates the value which it creates, which is greater than the value of the labor itself. Marx expressed this major thesis in *Das Kapital* in the following concise manner: 'The rule of capital over the worker is merely the rule of things over man, of dead over live labor.'[4]

The specific historical form which made possible the appropriation of objectified labor in Marx's time was the use of capital as private property in the means of production. This specific feature obscured a fact of generality. It is no wonder that to many Marxists it still seems that allowing the possibility of exploitation in a society in which private property as the means of production has been abolished is to allow a *contradiction in adjecto*. Nevertheless, it is obvious that private property as the means of production is not the only social institution which allows for the disposal of objectified labor. In a market economy during the transitional period this institution can be the monopolistic position of indi-

---

1 See K. Marx, *Economic and Philosophical Manuscripts*, in Erich Fromm, *Marx's Concept of Man*, New York, 1961, p. 108.
2 *Marx's Concept of Man*, p. 125.   3 Ibid., p. 126.
4 *Marx-Engels Archiv*, Moscow, 1933, p. 68.

vidual collectives, a position which enables them to sell their commodities above their value. Such collectives, in fact, appear in the market as collective capitalists and collective exploiters. (Needless to say, within the process of internal distribution this appropriated surplus of value will be assured of never reaching the pockets of the producers themselves. It will find its way to the bureaucratic and technocratic parts of the enterprise.) Second, there is the possibility of a monopoly over the decision-making in a statist system. To the degree to which a bureaucracy exists and takes the disposal of objectified labor into its own hands, rewarding itself with privileges, this is only another appropriation of the surplus value created by the working class.

The only way definitely to abolish exploitation is to create the conditions which will prevent objectified labor from ruling over live labor. Here, above all, *the right to dispose of objectified labor is a right of the producers themselves.*

Alienation in the field of material production entails a corresponding alienation in the field of social life, the state and politics. Politics is separated from economics, and society is divided into two opposite spheres. One is *civil society*, with all the egoism of the owner of commodities, and marked by envy, greed, and indifference towards the true needs of others. The other sphere is that of the *political society*, that of the abstract citizen who in an illusory way personifies the general interest of the community.

Kant and Hegel outlined two basic but contrary concepts of the state and law. Kant's starts from the real society, characterized by the market and by mutual competition among egotistic individuals, and attempts to reconcile the general interest with freedom of the individual in a negative manner, by demanding restriction of the self-initiative and arbitrariness of the individual. Hegel correctly perceived that simple common coexistence and mutual restriction of selfish individuals does not constitute a true human community. He therefore tried to transcend this negative relationship of one individual to another, seen as a limit, by the assumption of a rational citizen and also a rational community, in which community the individual relates positively to the social whole and through it to another individual. However, Hegel himself remained within the framework of bourgeois society, conceiving rationality as an abstract identification of the subjective spirit of the individual with the objective spirit of the state. The state as the personification of ideal human community is a pure abstraction which fictively transcends the existing empirical reality of bourgeois society.

In his criticism of Hegel's philosophy of law, Marx properly observed, first, that such a reduction of possible concrete human community to an abstract state, along with the reduction of a concrete, historically given individual to an abstract citizen, amounts to alienation in thought. Marx observed, second, that this alienation in thought is the result of alienation in reality itself. The German picture of the modern state was only possible because the state did abstract itself from true people and fulfilled the total man in only an imaginary way.[1]

In civil society, there is *bellum omnium contra omnes*, and only intersecting and mutually contradictory *separate* interests receive expression. In the political realm, the state-in-general appears as a necessary supplement, and in Hegel's conception it 'exists *an sich* and *für sich*.' The state, then, is an alienated universal and necessarily entails a certain formalism, namely bureaucracy. Bureaucracy attempts to affirm general interest as something special, *beside and above all other private and special interests*.[2] In that way it presents itself as an alienated social power which treats the world as a mere object of its activity. On the other hand, the state and bureaucracy are necessary supplements to the crumbling world of the owners of commodities, who follow only their special and private goals: the state supports a special interest but creates the illusion of its generality. 'General interest can be maintained in face of special interest only as something 'particular' in as much as the particular in face of the general is maintained as something general.'[3]

Needless to say, this dualism between the bureaucratized state and special private interest was impossible to resolve by identifying these contradictions in an imaginary way, within the framework of abstract thought.

'The abolition of bureaucracy,' says Marx, 'is possible onlywhen general interest becomes reality,' and when 'special interest really becomes *general* interest.'[4] And that is only possible when the individual man begins to live, work and relate to his fellow man in a human way. 'Only when man ceases to separate his *forces*

1 Marx, 'Kritik der Hegelschen Rechtsphilosophie,' in Marx and Engels, *Werke*, vol. 1, pp. 384–5.
2 Ibid., p. 297.
3 Ibid., p. 248.
4 Ibid., p. 250.

propres as a social power from himself in the form of political power, only then will human emancipation be achieved.'[1]

Marx explained this conception more clearly in *Grundrisse*. Here he compares political with religious alienation. In both cases man projects his general human characteristics and needs either into a supra-mundane being, or into the state. Either can be a necessary supplement to the incomplete social reality and can wither away only when man liberates himself from the idiocy of tying his entire life to one calling or to wage labor.

Marx shows in *Das Kapital* that all the basic rights guaranteed by the state to its citizens have a formal and alienated character. *Freedom* is merely the citizen's right to dispense of his commodity. *Equality* is in reality merely the application of the principle of equality to the exchange of commodity.[2] Everyone looks out for himself and not for the other. General good can only be realized 'behind the back of the individual' by the 'invisible hand,' as Adam Smith says. For Marx, the question is how to strive for the general goals of the community consciously and freely, in the most rational and most human way. For this, the state is not necessary. 'Freedom consists in transforming the state from an organ which dominates society into an organ which is completely subordinate to it, and even at the present, the forms of the state are more or less free to the degree that they limit the freedom of the state.'[3]

In his early work, *The Poverty of Philosophy*, Marx offered the theory that[4]

in the process of its development the working class will replace the old civil society with an association which excludes classes and their contradictions. Then there will no longer be political rule in the traditional sense, because political rule is precisely the official expression for the class contradictions in civil society.

In the *Communist Manifesto* Marx says that achieving democracy is the first step in the workers' revolution. The state is nothing more than 'the proletariat organized as the ruling class.'

Marx's concept of the fate of the state during the revolution is particularly clear in his analysis of the Paris Commune. He talks throughout of 'destroying state rule,' of 'smashing' it, of its being 'superfluous.' With enthusiasm he accepts two 'infallible means,'

1 Marx, 'Zur Judenfrage,' in Marx and Engels, MEGA, vol. 1, 1, p. 599.
2 Marx, *Das Kapital*, Berlin, 1947, vol. 1, p. 184.
3 'Kritik des Gothaer Programms,' in Marx-Engels, *Werke*, 19:27.
4 Marx, MEGA, vol. 1, 6, p. 227.

as Engels calls them, for preventing bureaucratism. These were employed in the Commune. First, 'the Commune appointed for its officials persons elected by the general vote, persons who are directly responsible and at any time replaceable by their electors.' Second, 'public office, whether high or low position, had to be performed for worker's wages.'[1] For the first time in history, if only for a short period, the state was replaced by self-management.

At the time of his 'Paris Manuscripts' of 1844, it was not yet clear to Marx as to how to overcome alienated labor. He offers only a rough draft of the general vision of a society in which all individuals develop freely and realize themselves as complete personalities. He sees social relationships as no longer consisting of envy, competition, abuse and mutual indifference. They are relations in which the individual, fulfilling the needs of the next man and fulfilling and enrichening his own being, directly experiences his own affirmation and self-realization as a man.

Marx gives a concrete historical dimension to this general vision of a transcendence of alienated labor in his *Grundrisse*. It was clear to him that new, more humane relations of production can occur only in an advanced society. Production relations there, thanks to scientific and technological progress, have become universal, no matter how reified. Only when men are no longer directly governed by other men but by abstract forces, by reified social laws, will the possibility be created of bringing these reified conditions of existence under communal social control.

In *Das Kapital*, Marx's solution for the problem of alienation of labor is clearly outlined. There is, for example, the discussion of the fetishism of commodities:[2]

> The form of the process of social life, i.e. of the process of material production will cast off from itself the mystical foggy veil only when the product of freely associated people is under their conscious, planned control. But this requires a material basis and a set of material conditions which in themselves are the wild product of a long and painful history of development.

One should particularly underline the famous passage in the third volume of *Das Kapital* where Marx says:[3]

> Freedom in the field of material production cannot consist of any-

---

1 'Address to the General Council of International Workers Union concerning the Civil War in France,' in Marx-Engels, *Werke*, 17:339.
2 Marx, *Das Kapital*, vol. 1, ch. 1, sec. 4.
3 Ibid., vol. 3, ch. 48, sec. 2.

thing else but the fact that socialized men, associated producers, regulate their interchange with nature rationally, bring it under their common control instead of being ruled by it as by some blind power; that they accomplish their task with the least expenditure of energy and under conditions most adequate to their human nature and most worthy of it.

The idea of self-management is also enriched and made concrete through Marx's analyses of the Paris Commune. All the elements of self-management are given.

1 The regulation of the process of labor is to be left in the hands of the workers themselves. It cannot remain the monopoly of any special profession of managers who concern themselves with it only. They, as the only historical subjects, will manipulate all other people as objects.

2 Producers must be *associated*, and their association must be *free*. Self-management is not, therefore, the atomization and disintegration of society, as some of its opponents represent it and as it may appear in practice when mistakenly understood. Self-management assumes integration and this integration is free and voluntary.

3 The control of production carried out by the associated producers must be *conscious* and *planned*. The exchange with nature must be regulated in a *rational manner*, and not abandoned to the rule of blind powers. Self-management, therefore, assumes constant direction, the elimination of uncontrolled economic forces. This presupposes the development of culture and science, and a clear understanding of the goals of development. Without this it is useless to speak of rationality.

4 This communal control and direction of material production should engage as little human energy as possible. Managing things, and above all managing people, cannot be a goal in itself, but can only be a means for securing truly free, creative and spontaneous activity.

5 The kind of self-management which Marx had in mind is only possible given a relatively high degree of development in a society. Among other things, it 'requires the kind of material basis which is the result of the long and painful history of development.' However, initial incomplete forms, even when abortive, offer important experience. For this reason Marx investigated so seriously and with such interest the experience of the Paris Commune and derived conclusions from it for the practice of the workers' move-

ment. For this reason history will certainly justify efforts in Yugo-
slavia to begin the introduction of the initial forms of self-management, even if in unripe conditions.

6   In describing the conditions under which the exchange with
nature takes place, Marx does not consider success and efficiency,
the increase in power over nature, great material wealth, as the
most important things. For him, the most important thing is that
the process goes forward under conditions which are the *most
adequate and the most worthy of the human nature of the worker*.

Marx thus concludes the third volume of *Das Kapital* with the
same humanist ideas advanced in his early writings, especially in
Economic and Philosophical Manuscripts. Self-management, far
from being one among several alternative principles of organization, is a necessary condition of a new genuinely socialist society.
It is the form of socialist democracy and radical human emancipation.

3   The feasibility of self-management

What most critics of self-management challenge is not so much
its desirability as its feasibility.

The customary objection against self-management is that such a
system is incompatible with the demands of technological efficiency
and rationality in a complex industrial society. Self-management is
a noble humanitarian idea but it cannot be realized because
workers and ordinary citizens are incapable of running a modern
economy and a modern state. Professional experts are needed to do
the job. In modern society it is important that decisions are taken
by persons equipped for that function by technical and other
knowledge and skill rather than by persons merely elected in the
hope that they will express the needs of the people. Consequently
self-management is either utopian or it must be reduced to a limited
participation of workers in the decision-making process.

There are several ways in which a humanist philosopher may
respond to the argument of efficiency.

He can argue that beyond a certain high level of technological,
economical and cultural development, efficiency begins to lose its
importance. After all, efficiency in its present-day meaning is
ability to produce a desired result, to carry out a defined task in
the social division of labor. In a highly developed future society,
automata will increasingly replace man in routine physical and

intellectual operations. Man will let computers be efficient, and he will engage more and more in the production of *unique, beautiful* objects, and in playing *new, surprising,* hitherto undefined roles. He will, that is, engage in *praxis,* and in *praxis* the question of efficiency does not arise at all, or is of secondary importance.

It may be argued, further, that the concept of efficiency is devoid of any humanist meaning. It is only apparently value-free and ideologically neutral. On closer scrutiny, it turns out to be ideologically loaded and to encapsulate certain harmful and dangerous attitudes toward nature and existing society. Maximum efficiency in conquering and controlling natural surroundings means a dangerously growing rate of waste of material resources and energy. Maximum efficiency in running present-day social organizations and institutions means full-scale endorsement of their inhuman and degrading practices. For unjust systems efficiency is their best chance of survival.

Under given assumptions this critique is perfectly sound. In a highly developed future society, both material production and the maximization of efficiency will become social goods of secondary importance. They are, however, still the primary concern of every present-day society. Man will liberate himself from excessively defined and ordered roles in material production and will be able to relax about efficiency only when he masters it, when he is able to relegate it to machines. And even then there will be a desirable kind of efficiency, associated with achievement of goals of human activity, whatever these goals might be.

Therefore one must take seriously the problem of the compatibility of self-management and efficiency. While dozens of countries have an average income of one hundred dollars *per capita* or less, while poverty remains even in Europe and North America, and while human beings still spend their life energy in boring work, it is clear that a further increase in efficiency is a necessary condition of human liberation and self-realization.

Human liberation is certainly inconceivable without every individual having the right to participate in decision-making. But is it really the case that the full and meaningful participation of each citizen must destroy efficiency?

This will not happen if the following three groups of conditions are satisfied.

1 The first group of conditions follows analytically from the very concept of integral *self-management.* Workers' councils in the

enterprises and the councils of local communities are not isolated atoms but rather are elements of a whole network with different levels. The network is in part territorial, in part professional or industrial, and in each respect it has different levels.

Any individual has direct decision-making power in the basic units where he works and lives, and, in addition, has an indirect power at higher levels through his delegates. Any unit has the necessary autonomy and responsibility for decision-making on matters of its specific concern. There is also a readiness to co-operate and to harmonize interests with other units of the system. Higher-level organs of self-management must have the maximum possible understanding of the particular interest of each sub-system. They necessarily are vastly different from the organs of the state in so far as they are not instruments of any ruling élite, they do not oppress, and they do reduce interference to a minimum. In matters of common interest, however, after a certain policy has been widely discussed and accepted, its decisions must be binding. Otherwise social life lacks a minimum of necessary organization and coordination, and tends to disintegrate.

2 Another group of conditions follows from the general characteristics of self-determination discussed above. Organs of self-management operate in a society with the following features. Media of communication are free, and contribute to the creation of a genuinely democratic public opinion. Political parties in the classical sense are absent but there is a plurality of other forms of non-authoritarian and non-manipulative political organizations. There is an ongoing process of education and a raising of the socialist consciousness of all individuals.

3 The third group of conditions making for the reconciliation of self-management and efficiency derives from an analysis of the basic stages of decision-making and of the different kinds of knowledge and competence needed. Each rational technical decision presupposes (a) a critical analysis of the situation (including a scrutinizing of the effectiveness of past policies), (b) a long-range program of development, a set of basic goals with respect to which all concrete technical decisions constitute means. Thus there are seen to be three distinct functions in the process of rational decision-making: one is *fact-finding, analytical, and informative*. Another is *governing, political*. The third is *technical* and *managerial*. Accordingly there are three distinct kinds of knowledge relative to these functions: factual, theoretical knowledge; knowledge of the basic needs of people in a certain

situation; technical knowledge of the ways in which basic decisions can most effectively be realized. Thus, in addition to the organ of self-management, composed of wise and experienced persons who understand the basic needs of a given moment there must be a group of analysts concerned with the implementation of adopted programs and with changes in external and internal factors, and, finally, a group concerned with technical management. This latter group will elaborate concrete alternative policy proposals, and try to realize decisions of the organ of self-management in the most efficient possible way.

In this complex structure, technocratic tendencies are the main danger to self-management. (To be sure, while there is still a state and a ruling party, much greater danger comes from political bureaucracy. However, we are now discussing a model of highly developed, integrated self-management in which the functions of the traditional state and authoritarian party have been taken over by the central organs of self-management.) A permanent source of technocratic tendencies is the fact that the managers hold executive power, and usually have better access to data. They may therefore try to manipulate the self-managing council. Excessive power of the managers is dangerous since their understanding of social needs may be very limited and their scale of values very biased. They may give priority to typically instrumental values of growth, expansion and order. Contrary to a common prejudice that modern society requires the rule of experts, the truth appears to be that experts are least qualified to be rulers, precisely because they are only experts and their rationality is merely technical.

Self-management has at least three defenses against manipulation by the technostructure: 1 independent access to data; 2 the iron rule that the management prepares its proposals for the organ of self-management in the form of wide alternatives among which to choose; 3 the right to elect, reelect or replace managers.

The organ of self-management must have its own informative and analytic service, and not depend on managers. Otherwise, it will be at the mercy of half-truths. The organ of self-management must, time and again, assert its right of decision-making. If it is reduced to an institution which merely votes on the proposals prepared by the management, it becomes a victim of manipulation. In order to keep the balance and to be able to assert its rights, the organ of self-management must have the power of rotating managers. There is no real danger that a 'primitive' or 'ignorant' workers' council will sack a good and efficient manager. The experience of Yugoslav self-management suggests that if the workers' council sacks a manager this is because he is utterly incompetent or because he is too authoritarian or because he is both. The real danger is that the workers use this right too rarely or too late, after considerable damage has already been done. This reluctance to react promptly indicates that what jeopardizes the efficiency of production in socialism is too little rather than too much of workers' participation.

Self-management has the historical opportunity to supplant those irrational and truly wasteful forms of society which rest on capital and the market and on authoritarian political machines.

9 Stalinist Party-commitment and Communist Dignity

SVETOZAR STOJANOVIĆ

This paper is concerned with one theme of a number of related ones dealing with the dignity of man. Its concern is the dignity of the communist. However, it is not about the dignity of the communist in his relationship to the enemies of the revolution. On this point, there has never been any doubt except, of course, from the practical point of view: can the communist gather enough physical strength to maintain his defiant dignity when in the hands of the counterrevolutionary terror? We shall here be concerned with something else, the attitude of the communist towards his party. This relationship has remained, both theoretically and practically, outside of the Marxists' realm of interest. The reason for this has been the doctrine of unlimited party-commitment[1] predominant under Stalinism in almost all communist parties. The communist has been prepared for the conscious and complete submission of all that is individual – his interests, rights, views and actions – to the collective revolutionary endeavour. Readiness not only for an heroic sacrifice, but for the complete oblivion of his self as well, has been expected from the communist.

But does not such party-commitment belong exclusively to the past? The Bendit brothers, in *Obsolete Communism: The Left-Wing Alternative*, express their belief that the time when revolutions demanded sacrifices is gone and that we are now heading for a time when revolutions will be inseparable from joy and pleasure. The prediction is too good to be believed. The old world's power and determination have not decreased to such an extent. Sacrifice will for long continue to be an inseparable part of the revolutionary effort. To come to the main point, some revolutionaries in the future will live and die with the belief that it is their duty to sacrifice *everything* they have to the revolution, including all personal dignity.

The horrifying discoveries of the nature of Stalinism have shown to what extent and by what means a large part of the communist

---

1 'Party-commitment' is an approximate translation of 'partiinost' and its exact German translation, 'Parteilichkeit'.

movement has abused the unselfish readiness of communists to sacrifice themselves. We have recently been ruthlessly reminded, by the Cuban poet Padilla's public self-criticism and repentance, that these discoveries by themselves do not provide any guarantee against repetition in history:[1]

> I am moved by a sincere desire to make amends, to compensate the Revolution for the harm I have occasioned, and to compenpensate myself spiritually. I may prevent others from losing themselves stupidly .... Under the disguise of the writer in revolt within a socialist society, I hid opposition to the Revolution; behind the ostentation of the critical poet who paraded his sickly irony, the only thing I really sought was to persist in my counterrevolutionary hostility. Among both Cubans and foreigners, I discredited every one of the initiatives of the Revolution, striving to look like an intellectual who was an expert in problems ... I in fact knew nothing about. Following this course I committed grave faults against the true intellectual's moral code, and what is worse, against the Revolution itself.

1   Self-humiliation under the guise of revolutionary unselfishness

A man who has not dedicated himself to a revolutionary cause, and is the victim of certain onslaughts, may be able to preserve a minimum of his dignity, or at least an illusion of it, by retreating into his self. His mute and non-engaged existence will provide a shelter from the waves which threaten completely to destroy his ego. But, since the dignity of the communist is not contemplative but active, it cannot be preserved and lived out in the form of a purely interior experience. That is why he must choose. He has either bravely to resist all attempts to make him bend his back, or to commit moral suicide by admitting his 'guilt' in self-criticism and repentance.

An 'ordinary' man will give in to the pressure *as pressure*. He has no need for self-rationalization in order to go on living after this humiliation. The communist who gives in to his party, however, must find some 'deep' justification for himself. If he does not, he will be crushed under the burden of his self-contempt.

The communist has one rationalization handy. He has heard that a feeling preventing the communist from giving in to the party is not an expression of real moral strength, but rather a remnant of

1 Quoted according to the *New York Times*, 26 May, 1971.

vanity, a petit-bourgeois-individualistic weakness. What is being asked of the communist is allegedly not self-humiliation, but rather real revolutionary unselfishness.

His situation is eased, so to speak, by another fact. The Stalinized communist has never prepared himself for a dignified confrontation with his comrades. On the contrary, he has been entirely taken up with almost obsessive self-examination of his personal readiness to endure heroically all the tortures to be suffered at the hands of the enemy. He has no strength left to maintain a dignified attitude toward his fellow-fighters. Such an attitude seems largely superfluous, since he has been taught that 'the right attitude towards the class enemy' is an heroic obstinacy, and 'the right attitude towards the party' is self-criticism. We have here an existence that is both revolutionary and split: someone who is a Prometheus in the face of the enemy easily becomes a weakling in the face of his party.

Intellectuals are particularly vulnerable in this respect, as they are often directed by an unconscious guilt-feeling due to their non-proletarian origin. They desire to prove at all costs their devotion to the 'cause of the proletariat' (a devotion which they tend to identify almost *a priori* with unlimited devotion to the party). Rare are those intellectuals who have managed to bring this guilt-feeling into consciousness and, as conscious, do away with it. Such intellectuals, instead of being ashamed of their origin, are rightly proud in that they have succeeded in overcoming, by their personal choice, the social determinism leading them in the direction of counter-revolution. They do not suffer from an inferiority feeling when faced with communists of proletarian origin, because they know that such communists had to make no such individual effort. Their very social position directed them to the side of the revolution.

2   The trap of 'objective' meaning and 'objective' guilt

In order really to acknowledge his 'guilt', the Stalinized communist must do more, of course, than simply suppress the feeling of personal dignity which is indeed an 'instinct' of moral self-preservation. He must also reach the conclusion that *in a way* he was really guilty. This, however, is not possible without the aid of a strict distinction between so-called objective and so-called subjective guilt. The communist is not, of course, required to confess that he has intentionally (subjectively) harmed the revolutionary cause and helped the enemy. That, of course, would be intolerable, as it would negate his elementary honesty as a communist. After that, only the honourable solution of suicide would be left to him. The Stalinized party also would gain nothing by this solution. Such a party is in need of fighters who will atone for their 'sins' by severe self-criticism and absolute discipline.

As a man of action, the communist *volens-nolens* takes responsibility from the very beginning not only for intended but also for (some) unintended consequences of his activity. The individual who intentionally interferes with the flow of history must reckon in advance with the difference between the subjective and objective meaning of his acts, and must therefore be prepared to take upon himself consequences due to both aspects. The subjective meaning is of course defined by the actor's intentions, while the objective meaning is far beyond these limits. Naturally the hardest question to answer is: just how far?

Even Merleau-Ponty, in his *Humanism and Terror*, was implicitly of the opinion that the revolutionary should be responsible for *all* the consequences of his revolutionary activity: intended and unintended, short-term consequences and those of the longest duration, the direct and the extremely indirect, the foreseeable and the unforeseeable. And, as history is ambiguous, this totality can never be finally defined, either quantitatively or qualitatively.

Something within ourselves spontaneously protests against this. It is, I think, an inhuman requirement. Is not such an understanding of objective meaning too unlimited to be attributed to any finite being, even the revolutionary? Apart from this, such potential infiniteness of objective meaning, as we shall presently see, makes possible the manipulation of the noble feeling of revolutionary responsibility.

By accepting this form of objectivity in order to transcend his subjectivity, the communist fighter in fact becomes caught in the web of party subjectivism. It is obvious that the consequences by themselves do not constitute the meaning of a human act. Someone must first evaluate and ascribe meaning to them. If that meaning is to be really objective, it must be the result of inquiry: consequences are to be precisely ascertained, compared with one another, and put in order according to their importance. Only then can meaning be defined. However, the procedure of representatives of the Stalinized party is exactly the opposite. From the total of real and possible consequences, they arbitrarily choose the most secondary and then, with a pretence of objective meaning, charge the accused.

Hence a complete alienation of meaning takes place. The term 'alienation' is not used here in the trivial sense, according to which a man *always* loses control over his acts, inasmuch as he inevitably produces certain *unintended* as well as intended consequences. The Stalinized communist completely gives up his autonomous right in the evaluation of the objective meaning of his own acts, and fully delegates this right to the Stalinized party. The inevitable result is that in the ruins of the individual subject there is raised up a collective subject with its pseudo-objectivity. There can be no effective defence against the alienation of the party so long as its members treat it as something greater than the totality of their organized revolutionary activity.

This abdication of the individual subject before the Stalinized party's subjectivism also has another side. In the throes of un-limited party-commitment, the Stalinized communist fails to notice that the leadership of a Stalinized party, when evaluating its own policies, acts in defiance of the principle of objective meaning. On such occasions, the leadership accents the intended consequen-ces of its activity. Accordingly, each change in party policy is explained and justified by a supposed alteration in objective circumstances, and not as a correction of mistakes committed.

In any case, it would not occur to the Stalinized communist, not to mention the leadership, to question the objective meaning (the consequences) of this conception of the 'objective' meaning. If it did occur to him, however, he would see objective meaning change from evidence condemning him into a charge against his prosecutor. It has become quite clear that mystification with 'objective' meaning has made an important contribution to the Stalinist degeneration of a large number of the communist parties.

3 *The metaphysical and the positivistic attitudes*

Until now we have seen how our Stalinized communist's unhappy consciousness is torn between dignity and humiliating self-criticism, as well as between the subjective and the objective meaning of his acts. His consciousness, however, is riven by still another fatal contradiction, that one involving the metaphysical and the positivistic attitude towards the party.

Even when cornered by the abundance of evidence of grave mistakes, injustices, deformations and even crimes in such a party, this communist still will not abandon the principle of absolute loyalty to the party. The peculiar metaphysics of the party provides him with a redeeming explanation and justification: whatever may happen within the party is not characteristic of the party *as such*. An *a priori* essence of the party remains for ever untouched, above all which is actual and potential in its empirical life. Klement Gotwald, when some Czechoslovakian Communist Party members asked him whom they could trust after the 'treason' of Slansky and other leaders replied: Trust the Party!

Without such a metaphysical guarantee, the Stalinized communist, who has not been sufficiently prepared to sustain himself, would be devoid of his ideals, his mission, the meaning of his struggle. On first thought, one would expect that this *separation* of the metaphysical and the empirical would not only save such a communist from the abyss of hopelessness, but would also inspire him to resist the empirical when it conflicts with the metaphysical. But this does not happen. Whenever the Stalinized communist is faced with the dilemma of whether or not to give in to party pressure, he quickly *identifies* these two planes, and does so to the advantage of the empirical. In this way, the metaphysical guarantee does not save him at all from a wholly empirical capitulation. On the contrary, the existing party leadership always personifies for him the essence of the party. Therefore, unlimited loyalty to the revolutionary cause is easily transformed into absolute obedience to those who have come out on top in the intra-party struggle for power. In connection with this, it may be useful to remember how the present super-empirical leadership of the Czechoslovakian Communist Party, imposed by external intervention, has in the name of the transcendental dimension of the party essentially changed the composition of the party membership by means of mass purges.

4 The omnipresent enemy

The unhappy consciousness we are discussing constantly adjusts itself to a metaphysical view of history which determines *a priori* the objective meaning of all revolutionary acts. These acts assume their meaning only when placed in the frame of this historical scheme and its basic factors and forces, taken as settled *a priori*.

The party as a subject in history represents an absolutely firm point in relation to which *everything* else *may* be defined as an anti-subject. There is no escape from the closed circle of this mani-chaeian polarization. The very thought of resisting a Stalinized party in the name of the preservation of personal dignity disinte-grates when faced with the above-mentioned concept of 'objective' meaning. Either you capitulate to the party or you *once more* help the enemy of the revolution. It may be added, parenthetically, that the bourgeoisie in its struggle against communism has deftly inverted and used that false dilemma. Either (our) democracy or Stalinism.

Solzhenitsyn has formulated nicely the most important element of Stalinism's constant evocation of the enemy. 'The enemies, eternal and ever-present, provide an easy justification for your functions and for your very existence. But what would you do without enemies? You could not survive without enemies.'[1] Of course, this obsession with the enemy in the communist movement began long before Stalinism. At first it took a much more innocent form. From Bebel to our present day, revolutionaries have lived in fear of somehow being praised by the enemy. The real tragedy came with Stalinism, when the enemy was found everywhere – to the left and to the right, close to and far away from the strict party line. Thus a situation was created in which the communist could not, by definition, take a single step away from that line without allegedly being of objective use to the enemy. The underlying principle is that even the most minute disagreement within the party may start a crack which the enemy can easily open into a huge gap. To prevent this, the Stalinist party has introduced a strict division of labour: the leadership takes upon itself the defining of the party line, leaving it to members to worry about how not to help the enemy objectively.

We all know, however, that man does not act in a vacuum. He cannot make a single move without someone undesirable benefiting from it to a certain extent. Using this ambiguity inherent to the human situation as such, the leadership of Stalinized parties can simultaneously press essentially contradictory charges. An example of this is the charge that over-zealousness in the realization of the leadership's decision can serve the enemy as much as the sabotage of its policies. The communist's dignity is threatened by a quite peculiar dialectic. 'The leftist deviation' meets the 'rightist

1 Letter to the Writers' Union, November 1969.

deviation'. But 'Extremes meet', as Huxley remarked, 'for the good reason that they were made to meet.'[1]

5　Chain reaction

The very first degrading act of the Stalinized communist opens a moral gap which is quick to widen. This essential step is hardest to make. Any further weakness is a matter of degree rather than principle. After this step is taken, all the remaining defences fall like dominoes. Those who reckon that they will be able to avoid further party demands by the 'cunning' of petty self-criticism are gravely mistaken. Moloch is insatiable. Bowing down to him provokes his immediate scorn, and, at the same time, a demand for complete capitulation.

The cumulative effect of the surrender, of course, does not issue solely in one's getting accustomed to self-humiliation. As he has not had enough strength to resist, the Stalinized communist will in future attack with all his strength, almost sadistically, all those who do offer real resistance. He will do so because, as long as there are communists who by their behaviour remind him of his unrealized human possibilities, he will not be able completely to suppress shame. The object of contempt, hatred and destruction is unconsciously transformed from being the Stalinized party prosecutor and also one's own self, and becomes those communists who are jealously guarding their moral integrity.

There is the fateful question of who will serve as a model of the right attitude not only to the enemy, but also to the party. The extent of the danger of a dignified stance being taken to the communist party is best gauged by the degree of insistence on the breaking down of the communist's personality. Those in power have always remained extremely dissatisfied if excommunications were not followed by the self-humiliation. The reason has been that they have instinctively felt that control over men is complete only when their dignity, the value-nucleus of the personality, is overcome. The real purpose of the Stalinist trials was not the physical extermination of the accused and general deterrence, which could have been achieved without the public shows. It was the gaining of satisfaction from communist revolutionaries' self-degradation. Only when the accused were made to show that they had no remaining strength did they become completely harmless.

1 *Brave New World*, New York, 1950, p. 45.

6   *The reserve sanction: subjective guilt*

In many cases, the charge of objective guilt has been effective enough. But on some occasions it has been necessary to resort to the charge of intentional harm caused to the revolutionary movement. This charge no longer implies neglect, lack of vigilance, inherited bourgeois prejudices, etc., but rather a conscious hostility. Many have noted that Bukharin, when he could not act as a real revolutionary (and so unmask the whole trial), nevertheless consistently insisted upon the fundamental difference between objective and subjective guilt. By his staunch denial of the latter, he tried to preserve the elementary honour of a revolutionary and a man.

Gramsci wrote:[1]

> The question arises whether it is honest to look into someone's past for all mistakes committed in order to reproach him with them for the purposes of the present polemic? Is it not human to err? Have not the big personalities in science been formed through their mistakes? Is not everyone's biography, to a great extent, a struggle against and then the overcoming of one's past?

What would Gransci have said if he had lived to see the monstrous Stalinist trials which, of course, did not deal in 'mistakes' but in the 'treason' of the great revolutionaries? By extending the technique described by Gramsci, the roots of treason have been 'found' far back in the revolutionaries' lives. Since, according to this conception, the present can always shed an essentially new light on to the revolutionaries' biographies, their lives can be transferred, by a single stroke, from the history of revolution to the history of counter-revolution.

7   *Personal dignity as the limit of revolutionary self-sacrifice*

In order to fulfil their mission, communist revolutionaries in despotic countries have had to gather into parties characterized by high concentration and unity of the will, strivings, action and self-sacrifice. In their struggle not even their lives have been sacrosanct. But their dignity has had to remain inviolable. Revolutionaries

1 *Il Materialismo storico e la filosofia di Benedetto Croce*, Rome, 1966, p. 279.

cannot sacrifice their dignity to the revolutionary cause, since it is inseparable from the moral nucleus of the personality.

If the ultimate sense of revolutionary self-sacrifice is to be sought in the creation of a society which will enable the full development of the human personality, it must, from the very beginning, carry within itself a conscious *personalistic* self-limitation and self-warrant. In this respect, the dignity of the communist represents the absolute minimum. The revolutionary cause and the dignity of the revolutionary cannot, even temporarily, be in relationship of higher and lower values in the axiological hierarchy. Personal dignity is an inseparable element of the revolutionary goals and ideals. The revolutionary fighter can sacrifice at this altar his life, but not his moral personality. 'An idea, in order to be able to change the world, has first to change the life of the man who carries it. It has to become an example.'[1]

The communist, by his heroic idealism, will make a real contribution in the realm of value only if he constantly guards his own dignity. By consenting to sacrifice his dignity and thus to negate his own moral value, he puts in question the moral meaning of all his sacrifices, past and future. Man is the carrier, the centre and the realizer of values. He cannot be worthy of the revolutionary cause if he himself has no dignity.

To preserve one's dignity – that is the duty of a communist not only to himself but also to the revolution. A social movement, if it is to preserve a revolutionary character, must never threaten the personal dignity of its members. Only a party made up of proud men has a secure revolutionary future. For this reason, it must always firmly resist the perverted and masochistic unselfishness of some of its fighters. At times it will appear that the revolutionary programme is not fully realizable. It would, however, be a dangerous illusion to find the smallest reason for this in the unreadiness of communists to sacrifice their personal dignity to the revolutionary cause.

The relationship of a communist and his party must be governed by the principle of *complete mutuality:* the mutuality of respect, solidarity, loyalty, and recognition. In this relationship there is room for the self-critical attitude, but not more room than there is for real criticism of the party. I say *real* criticism, because the Stalinized situation has been characterized by a pseudo-symmetry: unlimited self-criticism as against only hierarchical criticism. Is it necessary to add that self-critical attitude must be on guard

1 Albert Camus, *The Rebel.*

against even the faintest traces of humiliation, as well as be absolutely voluntary, and be such as to be practical and directed toward the future?

To stand upright before one's co-fighters is of course not an easy act for many, as they must abandon the illusion that the communist can be in the right only when he is with the party. If the communist does not keep an upright stance, he is more used by the party than he participates in it. Marx's categorical imperative 'to overthrow all conditions in which man is a degraded, enslaved, neglected, contemptible being'[1] must apply in the first instance to communists themselves.

1 'Toward the Critique of Hegel's Philosophy of Law: Introduction' (*Writings of the Young Marx on Philosophy and Society*, ed. L. D. Easton, K. H. Guddat, pp. 257–8).